FANTASTIC

POCKET
BIBLE
TRIVIA

QUESTIONS,
PUZZLES &
QUIZZES

TIMOTHY E. PARKER

SPIRE

© 2016 by Timothy E. Parker

Published by Revell
a division of Baker Publishing Group
Grand Rapids, Michigan
www.revellbooks.com

Spire edition published 2023
ISBN 978-0-8007-4303-1 (paperback)
ISBN 978-1-4934-4139-6 (ebook)

All material in this edition was published in 2016 by Revell in *The Official Bible Brilliant Trivia Book*.

Printed in the United States of America

Scripture quotations are from the King James Version of the Bible.

Baker Publishing Group publications use paper produced from sustainable forestry practices and post-consumer waste whenever possible.

23   24   25   26   27   28   29   7   6   5   4   3   2   1

Contents

Before You Begin

It is time to become brilliant in the knowledge of God's Word, the richness of the biblical past and the prophetic future. To get the true benefits of this book, you may have to go through it more than once. The goal is to challenge you in multiple ways, using multiple strategies and a wide array of exercises, puzzles, and quizzes, to get you to the highest level of Bible knowledge, a level I call Bible brilliant.

Joshua 1:8 states, "This book of the law shall not depart out of thy mouth; but thou shalt meditate therein day and night, that thou mayest observe to do according to all that is written therein: for then thou shalt make thy way prosperous, and then thou shalt have good success." Although this book uses clever games, word play, and trivia to increase your overall Bible knowledge, its goal is no trivial matter. It behooves every believer to know as much about the Lord and his Word as humanly possible. This book will be overwhelmingly helpful in that endeavor.

It is far more important for you to learn and know the information in the exercises than to complete the exercises quickly. In fact, I strongly recommend that you never time yourself in any challenge presented but take your time and focus on retaining correct answers.

This is an open-book book. That means you may use your own Bible to find answers. It is always a good thing to have the Good Book open, and you are never penalized in any way for referencing your own Bible as you seek answers to the thousands of questions presented.

Some of the exercises are easy, and some are maddeningly difficult. However, they all have one purpose, and that is to teach the Word of God and bring you to the highest levels of Bible understanding and true knowledge.

SECTION 1

THE MUST-KNOW SECTION

This section deals with Bible information, facts, and questions and answers that you absolutely must know to become Bible brilliant. (Answers begin on page 207.)

> All human discoveries seem to be made only for the purpose of confirming more and more strongly the truths contained in the sacred Scriptures.
>
> Sir William Herschel

Did You Know?
(SET 1)

Here are some facts that amaze.

- The youngest book of the Old Testament is the book of Malachi, written approximately 400 BC.
- Delilah did not cut Samson's hair. She called someone else to do it (Judges 16:19).
- There is a city named Sin in the book of Ezekiel (30:15).
- Although ivory is mentioned thirteen times in the Bible, elephants, the source of the ivory, are not mentioned at all.
- The longest single sentence in the King James Bible features the genealogy of Jesus and spans sixteen verses from Luke 3:23 all the way through Luke 3:38.
- There are at least five women named Mary in the New Testament.
- An unidentified son of a prophet once told a man to strike him. The man refused to strike the prophet's son and was told that because he refused, he would be killed by a lion. He was indeed killed in a lion attack (1 Kings 20:35–36).

150 Key Verses

Knowing key Scripture passages is essential to becoming a Bible scholar. In this important exercise, you are given 150 verses with one key word missing. If you fill in the missing word correctly, you may reward yourself with 2 points.

1. Matthew 5:3
   Blessed are the poor in _____: for theirs is the kingdom of heaven.

2. Colossians 1:13
   Who hath delivered us from the power of _____, and hath translated us into the kingdom of his dear Son.

3. Luke 10:1
   After these things the LORD appointed other _____ also, and sent them two and two before his face into every city and place, whither he himself would come.

4. Luke 7:36
   And one of the _____ desired him that he would eat with him. And he went into the Pharisee's house, and sat down to meat.

5. Luke 1:7
   And they had no child, because that _____ was barren, and they both were now well stricken in years.

6. Isaiah 6:1
   In the year that king _____ died I saw also the LORD
   sitting upon a throne, high and lifted up, and his train
   filled the temple.

7. Revelation 20:11
   And I saw a great white _____, and him that sat on it,
   from whose face the earth and the heaven fled away; and
   there was found no place for them.

8. Romans 1:26
   For this cause God gave them up unto vile affections: for
   even their women did change the natural use into that
   which is against _____.

9. Mark 1:15
   And saying, The time is fulfilled, and the kingdom of God
   is at hand: _____ ye, and believe the gospel.

10. Leviticus 20:13
    If a man also lie with mankind, as he lieth with a woman,
    both of them have committed an _____: they shall
    surely be put to death; their blood shall be upon them.

11. Ephesians 5:21
    Submitting yourselves one to another in the fear of

    _____.

12. 1 Corinthians 6:19
    What? know ye not that your body is the _____ of
    the Holy Ghost which is in you, which ye have of God,
    and ye are not your own?

13. Luke 19:10
    For the Son of man is come to seek and to _____ that
    which was lost.

14. Matthew 28:20

    _____ them to observe all things whatsoever I have
    commanded you: and, lo, I am with you always, even unto
    the end of the world.

15. Luke 24:1

    Now upon the first day of the week, very early in the
    morning, they came unto the _____, bringing the
    spices which they had prepared, and certain others with
    them.

16. Hebrews 4:14

    Seeing then that we have a great high _____, that is
    passed into the heavens, Jesus the Son of God, let us hold
    fast our profession.

17. 2 Chronicles 7:14

    If my people, which are called by my _____, shall
    humble themselves, and pray, and seek my face, and turn
    from their wicked ways; then will I hear from heaven, and
    will forgive their sin, and will heal their land.

18. 1 John 3:2

    Beloved, now are we the sons of _____, and it doth
    not yet appear what we shall be: but we know that, when
    he shall appear, we shall be like him; for we shall see him
    as he is.

19. 1 Corinthians 15:1

    Moreover, brethren, I declare unto you the _____
    which I preached unto you, which also ye have received,
    and wherein ye stand.

20. John 14:12
    Verily, verily, I say unto you, He that believeth on me, the
    works that I do shall he do also; and greater works than
    these shall he do; because I go unto my _____.

21. Mark 1:14
    Now after that John was put in _____, Jesus came
    into Galilee, preaching the gospel of the kingdom of God.

22. 2 Timothy 3:1
    This know also, that in the last days perilous _____
    shall come.

23. John 15:16
    Ye have not chosen me, but I have chosen you, and
    ordained you, that ye should go and bring forth
    _____, and that your fruit should remain: that
    whatsoever ye shall ask of the Father in my name, he may
    give it you.

24. Exodus 20:3
    Thou shalt have no other _____ before me.

25. Acts 2:37
    Now when they heard this, they were pricked in their
    heart, and said unto _____ and to the rest of the
    apostles, Men and brethren, what shall we do?

26. Luke 23:34
    Then said Jesus, Father, _____ them; for they know
    not what they do. And they parted his raiment, and cast
    lots.

27. Matthew 7:12

Therefore all things whatsoever ye would that _____
should do to you, do ye even so to them: for this is the law
and the prophets.

28. Matthew 6:24

No man can serve two _____: for either he will hate
the one, and love the other; or else he will hold to the one,
and despise the other. Ye cannot serve God and mammon.

29. Matthew 6:1

Take heed that ye do not your alms before men, to be
seen of them: otherwise ye have no reward of your Father
which is in _____.

30. Mark 1:1

The beginning of the gospel of Jesus Christ, the
_____ of God.

31. Jeremiah 31:31

Behold, the days come, saith the LORD, that I will make
a new _____ with the house of Israel, and with the
house of Judah.

32. James 5:6

Ye have _____ and killed the just; and he doth not
resist you.

33. Philippians 4:19

But my God shall supply all your need according to his
_____ in glory by Christ Jesus.

34. Matthew 18:20

For where two or three are gathered together in my
_____, there am I in the midst of them.

35. Daniel 9:24

     Seventy weeks are determined upon thy people and upon thy holy city, to finish the transgression, and to make an end of _____, and to make reconciliation for iniquity, and to bring in everlasting righteousness, and to seal up the vision and prophecy, and to anoint the most Holy.

36. James 4:6

     But he giveth more grace. Wherefore he saith, God resisteth the _____, but giveth grace unto the humble.

37. Mark 16:17

     And these signs shall follow them that believe; In my name shall they cast out devils; they shall speak with new _____.

38. Revelation 19:11

     And I saw _____ opened, and behold a white horse; and he that sat upon him was called Faithful and True, and in righteousness he doth judge and make war.

39. Psalm 19:1

     The heavens declare the glory of God; and the _____ sheweth his handywork.

40. John 1:6

     There was a man sent from God, whose name was _____.

41. 1 Corinthians 10:13

     There hath no _____ taken you but such as is common to man: but God is faithful, who will not suffer you to be tempted above that ye are able; but will with the temptation also make a way to escape, that ye may be able to bear it.

42. Luke 6:27

    But I say unto you which hear, Love your _____, do good to them which hate you.

43. Matthew 24:14

    And this gospel of the kingdom shall be preached in all the world for a witness unto all nations; and then shall the _____ come.

44. Matthew 4:4

    But he answered and said, It is _____, Man shall not live by bread alone, but by every word that proceedeth out of the mouth of God.

45. 2 Timothy 3:15

    And that from a child thou hast known the holy scriptures, which are able to make thee _____ unto salvation through faith which is in Christ Jesus.

46. Acts 5:3

    But Peter said, Ananias, why hath _____ filled thine heart to lie to the Holy Ghost, and to keep back part of the price of the land?

47. Matthew 5:38

    Ye have heard that it hath been said, An eye for an eye, and a tooth for a _____.

48. Colossians 2:9

    For in _____ dwelleth all the fulness of the Godhead bodily.

49. Colossians 2:8

    Beware lest any man spoil you through philosophy and vain deceit, after the tradition of men, after the rudiments of the _____, and not after Christ.

50. Galatians 6:1

    Brethren, if a man be overtaken in a fault, ye which are
    spiritual, restore such an one in the spirit of meekness;
    considering thyself, lest thou also be _____.

51. John 1:11

    He came unto his own, and his own _____ him not.

52. Hebrews 12:14

    Follow _____ with all men, and holiness, without
    which no man shall see the Lord.

53. John 3:19

    And this is the condemnation, that _____ is come
    into the world, and men loved darkness rather than light,
    because their deeds were evil.

54. Mark 12:30

    And thou shalt love the Lord thy God with all thy heart,
    and with all thy _____, and with all thy mind, and
    with all thy strength: this is the first commandment.

55. Daniel 9:27

    And he shall confirm the covenant with many for
    one week: and in the midst of the week he shall cause
    the sacrifice and the oblation to cease, and for the
    overspreading of _____ he shall make it desolate,
    even until the consummation, and that determined shall
    be poured upon the desolate.

56. Ecclesiastes 3:1

    To every thing there is a _____, and a time to every
    purpose under the heaven.

57. Acts 2:17

    And it shall come to pass in the last days, saith God, I will
    pour out of my Spirit upon all flesh: and your sons and
    your daughters shall _____, and your young men
    shall see visions, and your old men shall dream dreams.

58. Acts 1:4

    And, being assembled together with them, commanded
    them that they should not depart from _____, but
    wait for the promise of the Father, which, saith he, ye have
    heard of me.

59. Luke 1:10

    And the whole multitude of the people were praying
    without at the time of _____.

60. Philippians 2:6

    Who, being in the form of God, thought it not robbery to
    be _____ with God.

61. Matthew 1:23

    Behold, a _____ shall be with child, and shall bring
    forth a son, and they shall call his name Emmanuel, which
    being interpreted is, God with us.

62. Philippians 4:4

    _____ in the Lord always: and again I say, Rejoice.

63. Luke 12:14

    And he said unto him, Man, who made me a _____
    or a divider over you?

64. Luke 6:38

    Give, and it shall be given unto you; good measure, pressed
    down, and shaken together, and running over, shall men
    give into your _____. For with the same measure that
    ye mete withal it shall be measured to you again.

65. Romans 3:21
    But now the righteousness of God without the _____
    is manifested, being witnessed by the law and the
    prophets.

66. John 13:35
    By this shall all men know that ye are my disciples, if ye
    have _____ one to another.

67. Romans 15:4
    For whatsoever things were written aforetime were
    written for our learning, that we through patience and
    comfort of the _____ might have hope.

68. 1 John 4:8
    He that loveth not knoweth not God; for God is
    _____.

69. 1 John 2:2
    And he is the propitiation for our sins: and not for ours
    only, but also for the sins of the whole _____.

70. James 4:4
    Ye adulterers and adulteresses, know ye not that the
    friendship of the world is enmity with God? whosoever
    therefore will be a friend of the world is the _____ of
    God.

71. 1 Thessalonians 4:16
    For the Lord himself shall descend from heaven with
    a shout, with the voice of the archangel, and with the
    _____ of God: and the dead in Christ shall rise first.

72. 1 Corinthians 1:18
    For the preaching of the _____ is to them that perish
    foolishness; but unto us which are saved it is the power of
    God.

73. John 15:12

    This is my _____, That ye love one another, as I have loved you.

74. 2 Timothy 1:2

    To _____, my dearly beloved son: Grace, mercy, and peace, from God the Father and Christ Jesus our Lord.

75. 1 Corinthians 13:1

    Though I speak with the _____ of men and of angels, and have not charity, I am become as sounding brass, or a tinkling cymbal.

76. Job 1:6

    Now there was a day when the sons of God came to present themselves before the LORD, and _____ came also among them.

77. James 1:13

    Let no man say when he is _____, I am tempted of God: for God cannot be tempted with evil, neither tempteth he any man.

78. 1 Timothy 4:1

    Now the _____ speaketh expressly, that in the latter times some shall depart from the faith, giving heed to seducing spirits, and doctrines of devils.

79. Ephesians 2:19

    Now therefore ye are no more strangers and foreigners, but fellowcitizens with the saints, and of the _____ of God.

80. Acts 13:1

    Now there were in the church that was at _____ certain prophets and teachers; as Barnabas, and Simeon that was called Niger, and Lucius of Cyrene, and Manaen, which had been brought up with Herod the tetrarch, and Saul.

81. John 10:28

    And I give unto them eternal life; and they shall never _____, neither shall any man pluck them out of my hand.

82. James 1:19

    Wherefore, my beloved brethren, let every man be swift to hear, slow to speak, slow to _____.

83. Galatians 1:6

    I marvel that ye are so soon removed from him that called you into the grace of _____ unto another gospel.

84. Acts 10:38

    How God anointed Jesus of Nazareth with the Holy Ghost and with _____; who went about doing good, and healing all that were oppressed of the devil; for God was with him.

85. 2 Peter 1:3

    According as his divine power hath given unto us all things that pertain unto life and _____, through the knowledge of him that hath called us to glory and virtue.

86. Hebrews 11:12

    Therefore sprang there even of one, and him as good as _____, so many as the stars of the sky in multitude, and as the sand which is by the sea shore innumerable.

87. Acts 8:26

    And the angel of the Lord spake unto _____, saying,
    Arise, and go toward the south unto the way that goeth
    down from Jerusalem unto Gaza, which is desert.

88. Luke 22:19

    And he took _____, and gave thanks, and brake it,
    and gave unto them, saying, This is my body which is
    given for you: this do in remembrance of me.

89. Luke 5:1

    And it came to pass, that, as the people pressed upon him
    to hear the _____ of God, he stood by the lake of
    Gennesaret.

90. Colossians 1:18

    And he is the head of the body, the _____: who is the
    beginning, the firstborn from the dead; that in all things
    he might have the preeminence.

91. John 2:3

    And when they wanted wine, the _____ of Jesus saith
    unto him, They have no wine.

92. 1 Corinthians 12:12

    For as the body is one, and hath many members, and all
    the members of that one body, being many, are one body:
    so also is _____.

93. Acts 5:29

    Then _____ and the other apostles answered and
    said, We ought to obey God rather than men.

94. Luke 13:3

    I tell you, Nay: but, except ye _____, ye shall all
    likewise perish.

95. Matthew 25:41
    Then shall he say also unto them on the left hand, Depart
    from me, ye cursed, into everlasting _____, prepared
    for the devil and his angels.

96. Matthew 1:1
    The book of the generation of Jesus Christ, the son of
    _____, the son of Abraham.

97. John 17:21
    That they all may be one; as thou, Father, art in me,
    and I in thee, that they also may be one in us: that the
    _____ may believe that thou hast sent me.

98. James 5:13
    Is any among you afflicted? let him _____. Is any
    merry? let him sing psalms.

99. James 1:12
    _____ is the man that endureth temptation: for when
    he is tried, he shall receive the crown of life, which the
    Lord hath promised to them that love him.

100. Romans 5:6
    For when we were yet without strength, in due time
    Christ died for the _____.

101. John 4:19
    The woman saith unto him, Sir, I perceive that thou art a
    _____.

102. 2 Timothy 1:7
    For God hath not given us the spirit of _____; but of
    power, and of love, and of a sound mind.

103. Matthew 25:14

   For the kingdom of heaven is as a man travelling into a
   far country, who called his own _____, and delivered
   unto them his goods.

104. James 2:19

   Thou believest that there is one _____; thou doest
   well: the devils also believe, and tremble.

105. Acts 1:6

   When they therefore were come together, they asked of
   him, saying, Lord, wilt thou at this time restore again the
   kingdom to _____?

106. Luke 18:9

   And he spake this parable unto certain which trusted
   in themselves that they were _____, and despised
   others.

107. Luke 13:10

   And he was teaching in one of the synagogues on the
   _____.

108. Isaiah 64:6

   But we are all as an _____ thing, and all our
   righteousnesses are as filthy rags; and we all do fade as a
   leaf; and our iniquities, like the wind, have taken us away.

109. Luke 6:7

   And the scribes and Pharisees watched him, whether he
   would heal on the _____ day; that they might find an
   accusation against him.

110. Genesis 1:31

   And God saw every thing that he had made, and, behold,
   it was very good. And the evening and the morning were
   the _____ day.

111. Acts 4:32

    And the multitude of them that believed were of one heart and of one soul: neither said any of them that ought of the things which he _____ was his own; but they had all things common.

112. Acts 2:36

    Therefore let all the house of Israel know assuredly, that God hath made the same _____, whom ye have crucified, both Lord and Christ.

113. Luke 24:44

    And he said unto them, These are the words which I spake unto you, while I was yet with you, that all things must be fulfilled, which were written in the law of _____, and in the prophets, and in the psalms, concerning me.

114. Luke 1:12

    And when Zacharias saw him, he was troubled, and _____ fell upon him.

115. Revelation 21:8

    But the fearful, and _____, and the abominable, and murderers, and whoremongers, and sorcerers, and idolaters, and all liars, shall have their part in the lake which burneth with fire and brimstone: which is the second death.

116. 2 Peter 2:1

    But there were false _____ also among the people, even as there shall be false teachers among you, who privily shall bring in damnable heresies, even denying the Lord that bought them, and bring upon themselves swift destruction.

117. James 1:7

    For let not that man think that he shall _____ any thing of the Lord.

118. Hebrews 7:25

    Wherefore he is able also to _____ them to the uttermost that come unto God by him, seeing he ever liveth to make intercession for them.

119. Mark 12:29

    And Jesus answered him, The first of all the commandments is, Hear, O _____; The Lord our God is one Lord.

120. John 18:36

    Jesus answered, My _____ is not of this world: if my kingdom were of this world, then would my servants fight, that I should not be delivered to the Jews: but now is my kingdom not from hence.

121. Psalm 1:1

    _____ is the man that walketh not in the counsel of the ungodly, nor standeth in the way of sinners, nor sitteth in the seat of the scornful.

122. Romans 12:3

    For I say, through the grace given unto me, to every man that is among you, not to think of himself more highly than he ought to think; but to think soberly, according as God hath dealt to every man the measure of _____.

123. John 15:7

    If ye abide in me, and my words abide in you, ye shall _____ what ye will, and it shall be done unto you.

124. Mark 16:9

    Now when Jesus was risen early the first day of the week,
    he appeared first to Mary Magdalene, out of whom he had
    cast _____ devils.

125. Matthew 28:1

    In the end of the sabbath, as it began to dawn toward the
    first day of the week, came Mary Magdalene and the other
    _____ to see the sepulchre.

126. John 14:9

    Jesus saith unto him, Have I been so long time with you,
    and yet hast thou not known me, Philip? he that hath seen
    me hath seen the Father; and how sayest thou then, Show
    us the _____?

127. John 4:18

    For thou hast had _____ husbands; and he whom
    thou now hast is not thy husband: in that saidst thou truly.

128. Mark 10:45

    For even the Son of man came not to be ministered unto,
    but to minister, and to give his life a _____ for many.

129. James 3:1

    My brethren, be not many _____, knowing that we
    shall receive the greater condemnation.

130. Acts 5:1

    But a certain man named _____, with Sapphira his
    wife, sold a possession.

131. John 6:8

    One of his disciples, _____, Simon Peter's brother,
    saith unto him.

132. Leviticus 19:18
    Thou shalt not avenge, nor bear any _____ against the children of thy people, but thou shalt love thy neighbour as thyself: I am the LORD.

133. John 19:30
    When Jesus therefore had received the vinegar, he said, It is finished: and he bowed his head, and gave up the _____.

134. Mark 16:1
    And when the sabbath was past, Mary Magdalene, and Mary the mother of James, and _____, had bought sweet spices, that they might come and anoint him.

135. 1 John 1:5
    This then is the message which we have heard of him, and declare unto you, that God is _____, and in him is no darkness at all.

136. Matthew 5:48
    Be ye therefore _____, even as your Father which is in heaven is perfect.

137. Philippians 3:20
    For our conversation is in _____; from whence also we look for the Saviour, the Lord Jesus Christ.

138. John 3:6
    That which is born of the _____ is flesh; and that which is born of the Spirit is spirit.

139. Matthew 10:34
    Think not that I am come to send peace on earth: I came not to send peace, but a _____.

140. Hosea 4:6

     My people are destroyed for lack of knowledge: because
     thou hast rejected _____, I will also reject thee, that
     thou shalt be no priest to me: seeing thou hast forgotten
     the law of thy God, I will also forget thy children.

141. Isaiah 53:6

     All we like sheep have gone astray; we have turned every
     one to his own way; and the LORD hath laid on him the
     _____ of us all.

142. James 1:11

     For the sun is no sooner risen with a burning heat, but
     it withereth the grass, and the flower thereof falleth, and
     the grace of the fashion of it perisheth: so also shall the
     _____ man fade away in his ways.

143. Acts 17:28

     For in him we live, and move, and have our being; as
     certain also of your own poets have said, For we are also
     his _____.

144. 1 Peter 4:10

     As every man hath received the gift, even so minister the
     same one to another, as good _____ of the manifold
     grace of God.

145. 1 Peter 3:5

     For after this manner in the old time the holy _____
     also, who trusted in God, adorned themselves, being in
     subjection unto their own husbands.

146. 1 Thessalonians 2:3

     For our exhortation was not of _____, nor of
     uncleanness, nor in guile.

147. Philippians 2:3

     Let nothing be done through strife or vainglory; but in lowliness of _____ let each esteem other better than themselves.

148. Ephesians 6:1

     Children, obey your _____ in the Lord: for this is right.

149. John 1:2

     The same was in the _____, with God.

150. Isaiah 55:8

     For my thoughts are not your _____, neither are your ways my ways, saith the LORD.

The Ten Plagues Inflicted on Egypt

To be Bible brilliant and not just Bible literate, you must have a thorough understanding of the ten plagues God inflicted on Egypt in Exodus 7:14–12:30. God sent the plagues as a warning that there is only one true God. The Egyptians worshiped a multitude of false gods, and the Lord used the plagues to prove that nothing worshiped in Egypt could save them from his demonstrative power.

This tutorial will explain the ten plagues and their order. This section concludes with seven fill-in-the-blank questions to test your knowledge of the ten plagues.

Plague 1: Water Turned into Blood

God turned water throughout Egypt into blood. Fish and river animals died, and the Nile River reeked. The account of the first plague is in Exodus 7:14–25.

Plague 2: Frogs

The Lord saturated the land of Egypt with an abundance of frogs. Later, in yet another display of his power, God supernaturally killed the frogs, filling Egypt with the stench of their death. The full account of the second plague is in Exodus 8:1–15.

Plague 3: Lice

God sent an infestation of the wingless, biting parasites known as lice. The infestation was so thick that, according to Exodus 8:17, "All the dust of the land became lice throughout all the land of Egypt." The full account is in Exodus 8:16–19.

Plague 4: Flies

God sent massive, intrusive swarms of flies upon Egypt. Flies covered the ground, harassed the people, and invaded all the Egyptian homes. To prove he was God alone and that this plague was only for Egyptians, no flies invaded Goshen, where God's people, the Israelites, lived. This account is in Exodus 8:20–32.

Plague 5: Death of Livestock

God killed Egypt's cattle, horses, donkeys, camels, oxen, and sheep during the fifth plague. No livestock of the Israelites died during this time. This plague is detailed in Exodus 9:1–7.

Plague 6: Boils

God sent the sixth plague to Egypt without any warning. The sixth plague resulted in festering boils on all the Egyptians and an incurable itch. The boils were so bad that Pharaoh's magicians could not stand before Moses. The account of this plague is in Exodus 9:8–12.

Plague 7: Hailstorm

God provided prior warning before unleashing the worst hailstorm in Egypt's existence. The entire account is in Exodus 9:13–34.

Plague 8: Locusts

God sent swarms of locusts into Egypt that were so dense the land became dark because of them. Yet no locusts intruded into Goshen, where the Israelites were safe from the infestation. The account is in Exodus 10:1–20.

Plague 9: Darkness

Darkness "which may be felt" covered Egypt for three days. The darkness was so intense that, according to Exodus 10:21–23, people could not see each other. The Israelites, however, enjoyed light as usual.

Plague 10: Death of All Firstborn

The firstborn of the Egyptian people and the firstborn of their beasts were slain in the tenth and final plague. All deaths occurred in a single night. To show a clear distinction between the Egyptians and God's beloved Israelites, the Lord said the Israelites' peace on that historically gruesome night would be so complete that not even an Israelite dog would bark at a person or animal. The account is in Exodus 11:1–8; 12:21–30.

In the following exercise, take your time and try to fill in the missing plagues in the lists. In each case, the list is in order. This will help you to learn not only the plagues but also the order in which they occurred. Give yourself 10 points for each of the twenty-eight blanks you fill in correctly.

1.
   1.
   2. Frogs
   3. Lice

2.
   4. Flies
   5.
   6. Boils

3.
   7. Hailstorm
   8. Locusts
   9.
   10. Death of all firstborn

4.
   1.
   2. Frogs
   3. Lice
   4.
   5.
   6. Boils
   7. Hailstorm
   8.
   9.
   10. Death of all firstborn

5.
   1. Water turned into blood
   2.
   3.
   4. Flies
   5. Death of livestock
   6.

7.
8. Locusts
9. Darkness
10. Death of all firstborn

6.
   1. Water turned into blood
   2.
   3.
   4.
   5. Death of livestock
   6.
   7.
   8. Locusts
   9.
   10. Death of all firstborn

You knew this was coming. Try to fill in each plague in the order in which it occurred.

7.
   1.
   2.
   3.
   4.
   5.
   6.
   7.
   8.
   9.
   10.

ALL ABOUT MONEY

In the following exercises that teach God's wisdom in money affairs, take the words under each Scripture passage and put them in the appropriate blanks. By studying which word goes into which blank, you will learn what God desires us to know about money. Give yourself 2 points for each passage you complete accurately.

Any repeats of passages throughout the various money topics are intentional.

The Love of Money

1. Mark 4:19
   And the cares of this _____, and the deceitfulness of
   _____, and the _____ of other things entering in,
   _____ the word, and it becometh _____.

   > unfruitful   world   lusts   riches   choke

2. Mark 8:36
   For what shall it _____ a man, if he shall gain the
   whole _____, and _____ his own _____?

   > soul   profit   world   lose

3. 1 Timothy 6:9–11
   But they that will be rich fall into _____ and a
   snare, and into many foolish and hurtful _____,
   which drown men in _____ and perdition. For the
   love of money is the root of all evil: which while some
   coveted after, they have erred from the faith, and pierced
   themselves through with many sorrows. But thou, O man
   of God, flee these things; and follow after _____,
   godliness, faith, love, _____, _____.

   > destruction   temptation   righteousness
   > lusts   meekness   patience

Being Truly Prosperous

1. Genesis 26:12
   Then Isaac sowed in that _____, and received in the
   same _____ an _____: and the LORD _____
   him.

   land   year   blessed   hundredfold

2. Genesis 39:3
   And his _____ saw that the LORD was with him, and
   that the _____ made all that he did to _____ in
   his _____.

   LORD   hand   master   prosper

3. Deuteronomy 8:18
   But thou shalt _____ the LORD thy God: for it is
   he that giveth thee _____ to get _____, that he
   may establish his _____ which he sware unto thy
   _____, as it is this day.

   fathers   wealth   power   remember   covenant

4. Deuteronomy 15:10
   _____ shalt surely give him, and thine heart shall not
   be _____ when thou givest unto him: because that
   for this thing the LORD thy God shall _____ thee
   in all thy _____, and in all that thou puttest thine
   _____ unto.

   bless   works   grieved   thou   hand

5. Deuteronomy 24:19

When thou cuttest down thine _____ in thy field,
and hast forgot a _____ in the field, thou shalt not go
again to _____ it: it shall be for the stranger, for the
fatherless, and for the widow: that the _____ thy God
may bless thee in all the _____ of thine hands.

> harvest   work   fetch   LORD   sheaf

6. Deuteronomy 30:8–10

And thou shalt return and obey the voice of the LORD,
and do all his commandments which I command thee this
day. And the LORD thy God will make thee plenteous in
every _____ of thine hand, in the fruit of thy body,
and in the fruit of thy _____, and in the fruit of thy
land, for good: for the LORD will again rejoice over thee
for good, as he rejoiced over thy _____: If thou shalt
hearken unto the _____ of the LORD thy God, to
keep his _____ and his statutes which are written in
this book of the law, and if thou turn unto the LORD thy
God with all thine heart, and with all thy _____.

> commandments   soul   cattle   work   voice   fathers

7. Joshua 1:8

This book of the law shall not depart out of thy
_____; but thou shalt meditate therein day and
_____, that thou mayest observe to do according to
all that is _____ therein: for then thou shalt make
thy way prosperous, and then thou shalt have good
_____.

> written   success   mouth   night

8. 1 Chronicles 22:12
   Only the _____ give thee wisdom and
   understanding, and give thee _____ concerning
   Israel, that thou mayest keep the _____ of the LORD
   thy _____.

   law   God   LORD   charge

9. 2 Chronicles 31:20
   And thus did _____ throughout all _____, and
   wrought that which was good and right and truth before
   the _____ his _____.

   Judah   LORD   God   Hezekiah

10. Psalm 1:1–3
    Blessed is the man that walketh not in the counsel of the
    _____, nor standeth in the way of sinners, nor sitteth
    in the seat of the _____. But his delight is in the law
    of the LORD; and in his law doth he meditate day and
    night. And he shall be like a _____ planted by the
    rivers of _____, that bringeth forth his fruit in his
    season; his leaf also shall not wither; and whatsoever he
    doeth shall _____.

    ungodly   tree   prosper   water   scornful

11. Psalm 35:27
    Let them shout for joy, and be glad, that favour my
    _____ cause: yea, let them say continually, Let
    the LORD be _____, which hath pleasure in the
    _____ of his _____.

    servant   magnified   righteous   prosperity

12. Jeremiah 17:8

    For he shall be as a _____ planted by the _____,
    and that spreadeth out her roots by the _____,
    and shall not see when heat cometh, but her leaf shall
    be _____; and shall not be careful in the year of
    _____, neither shall cease from yielding fruit.

    green   drought   waters   tree   river

13. Malachi 3:10

    Bring ye all the _____ into the storehouse, that there
    may be meat in mine _____, and prove me now
    herewith, saith the _____ of _____, if I will not
    open you the windows of _____, and pour you out a
    _____, that there shall not be room enough to receive
    it.

    blessing   LORD   hosts   house   tithes   heaven

14. 3 John 1:2

    _____, I wish above all things that thou mayest
    _____ and be in _____, even as thy _____
    prospereth.

    prosper   health   soul   beloved

Being a Good Steward over One's Money

1. Genesis 2:15
   And the LORD God _____ the _____, and put
   him into the _____ of _____ to dress it and to
   _____ it.

   > Eden garden man keep took

2. Deuteronomy 10:14
   _____, the _____ and the heaven of _____
   is the LORD's thy God, the _____ also, with all that
   therein is.

   > heavens earth heaven behold

3. Luke 12:42–44
   And the Lord said, Who then is that faithful and wise
   _____, whom his lord shall make _____ over his
   _____, to give them their portion of _____ in due
   season? Blessed is that _____, whom his lord when he
   cometh shall find so doing. Of a truth I say unto you, that
   he will make him ruler over all that he hath.

   > steward ruler household meat servant

4. Luke 12:47–48

   And that _____, which knew his lord's will, and prepared not himself, neither did according to his will, shall be beaten with many stripes. But he that knew not, and did commit things worthy of _____, shall be _____ with few stripes. For unto _____ much is given, of him shall be much required: and to whom men have _____ much, of him they will ask the more.

   committed   stripes   servant   whomsoever   beaten

5. Luke 16:9–11

   And I say unto you, Make to yourselves _____ of the mammon of unrighteousness; that, when ye fail, they may receive you into everlasting habitations. He that is faithful in that which is least is _____ also in much: and he that is _____ in the least is unjust also in much. If therefore ye have not been faithful in the unrighteous _____, who will commit to your trust the true _____?

   unjust   mammon   faithful   friends   riches

6. Romans 14:8

   For whether we live, we live unto the Lord; and whether we _____, we die unto the _____: whether we _____ therefore, or die, we are the _____.

   Lord's   die   live   Lord

Saving

1. Proverbs 21:5
   The _____ of the diligent _____ only to plenteousness; but of every one that is _____ only to _____.

   hasty   thoughts   tend   want

2. Proverbs 21:20
   There is _____ to be desired and _____ in the dwelling of the _____; but a foolish man _____ it up.

   oil   treasure   wise   spendeth

3. Proverbs 27:12
   A _____ man foreseeth the _____, and hideth himself; but the _____ pass on, and are _____.

   evil   prudent   punished   simple

4. Proverbs 30:25
   The ants are a _____ not strong, yet they prepare their meat in the _____.

   summer   people

5. 1 Corinthians 16:2
   Upon the first _____ of the _____ let every one of you lay by him in store, as _____ hath prospered him, that there be no _____ when I come.

   God   week   day   gatherings

Tithing

1. Genesis 14:20

   And blessed be the most high _____, which hath delivered _____ enemies into thy _____. And he gave him _____ of all.

   > thine   tithes   God   hand

2. Genesis 28:20–22

   And _____ vowed a vow, saying, If God will be with me, and will keep me in this way that I go, and will give me _____ to eat, and raiment to put on, So that I come again to my father's _____ in peace; then shall the LORD be my God: And this stone, which I have set for a _____, shall be God's house: and of all that thou shalt give me I will surely give the _____ unto thee.

   > house   tenth   bread   Jacob   pillar

3. Exodus 23:19

   The first of the _____ of thy _____ thou shalt bring into the _____ of the LORD thy God. Thou shalt not seethe a _____ in his mother's _____.

   > milk   land   firstfruits   house   kid

4. Leviticus 27:30

   And all the _____ of the _____, whether of the _____ of the land, or of the fruit of the tree, is the LORD's: it is holy unto the _____.

   > land   seed   LORD   tithe

5. Numbers 18:26

   Thus speak unto the _____, and say unto them,
   When ye take of the children of _____ the tithes
   which I have given you from them for your _____,
   then ye shall offer up an heave offering of it for the LORD,
   even a tenth part of the _____.

   tithe   Levites   Israel   inheritance

6. Deuteronomy 14:22–23

   Thou shalt truly _____ all the increase of thy seed,
   that the field bringeth forth _____ by year. And thou
   shalt eat before the LORD thy God, in the place which
   he shall choose to place his _____ there, the tithe
   of thy _____, of thy wine, and of thine oil, and the
   _____ of thy herds and of thy _____; that thou
   mayest learn to fear the LORD thy God always.

   year   tithe   flocks   firstlings   corn   name

7. Deuteronomy 14:28

   At the end of _____ _____ thou shalt bring forth
   all the tithe of thine _____ the same _____, and
   shalt lay it up within thy _____.

   increase   three   years   gates   year

8. Deuteronomy 26:12

   When thou hast made an end of _____ all the
   tithes of thine increase the third year, which is the year
   of tithing, and hast given it unto the _____, the
   _____, the _____, and the _____, that they
   may eat within thy gates, and be filled.

   widow   stranger   fatherless   Levite   tithing

9. 2 Chronicles 31:5

   And as soon as the _____ came abroad, the children of _____ brought in abundance the firstfruits of corn, _____, and oil, and honey, and of all the increase of the field; and the _____ of all things brought they in _____.

   > abundantly   tithe   commandment   Israel   wine

10. Nehemiah 10:38

    And the priest the son of _____ shall be with the _____, when the Levites take _____: and the Levites shall bring up the tithe of the tithes unto the _____ of our God, to the chambers, into the _____ house.

    > treasure   Aaron   Levites   house   tithes

11. Proverbs 3:9–10

    Honour the _____ with thy substance, and with the firstfruits of all thine increase: So shall thy _____ be filled with _____, and thy presses shall burst out with new _____.

    > plenty   LORD   wine   barns

12. Ezekiel 44:30

    And the first of all the _____ of all things, and every oblation of all, of every sort of your oblations, shall be the priest's: ye shall also give unto the _____ the first of your _____, that he may cause the _____ to rest in thine house.

    > priest   dough   firstfruits   blessing

13. Amos 4:4

    Come to _____, and transgress; at Gilgal multiply _____; and bring your _____ every morning, and your _____ after three years.

    transgression   sacrifices   Bethel   tithes

14. Malachi 3:8

    Will a man _____ God? Yet ye have _____ me. But ye say, Wherein have we robbed _____? In _____ and _____.

    robbed   rob   offerings   tithes   thee

15. Matthew 23:23

    Woe unto you, scribes and _____, hypocrites! for ye pay tithe of mint and anise and _____, and have omitted the _____ matters of the law, _____, mercy, and faith: these ought ye to have done, and not to leave the other _____.

    cummin   undone   weightier   Pharisees   judgment

16. 1 Corinthians 16:1–2

    Now concerning the collection for the _____, as I have given order to the _____ of _____, even so do ye. Upon the first day of the _____ let every one of you lay by him in store, as _____ hath prospered him, that there be no gatherings when I come.

    God   saints   churches   Galatia   week

17. Hebrews 7:4

    Now consider how great this _____ was, unto whom even the _____ _____ gave the tenth of the _____.

    spoils   patriarch   man   Abraham

Ultimate Success

1. Deuteronomy 30:9
   And the LORD thy God will make thee plenteous in every work of thine _____, in the fruit of thy body, and in the _____ of thy cattle, and in the fruit of thy land, for good: for the LORD will again _____ over thee for good, as he rejoiced over thy _____.

   fathers   rejoice   hand   fruit

2. Joshua 1:8
   This book of the law shall not depart out of thy _____; but thou shalt _____ therein day and _____, that thou mayest observe to do according to all that is written therein: for then thou shalt make thy way _____, and then thou shalt have good _____.

   prosperous   mouth   meditate   night   success

3. Nehemiah 2:20
   Then _____ I them, and said unto them, The God of _____, he will prosper us; therefore we his servants will arise and _____: but ye have no _____, nor right, nor memorial, in Jerusalem.

   build   portion   answered   heaven

4. Psalm 1:1–3
   Blessed is the man that _____ not in the counsel of the ungodly, nor standeth in the way of sinners, nor sitteth

in the seat of the scornful. But his _____ is in the law
of the LORD; and in his law doth he _____ day and
night. And he shall be like a tree planted by the _____
of water, that bringeth forth his fruit in his season; his leaf
also shall not _____; and whatsoever he doeth shall

_____.

prosper   rivers   wither   walketh   delight   meditate

5. Psalm 37:4
   Delight _____ also in the _____: and he shall
   give thee the _____ of thine _____.

   desires   thyself   heart   LORD

6. Proverbs 22:29
   Seest thou a _____ diligent in his _____? he shall
   stand before _____; he shall not stand before mean

   _____.

   men   business   kings   man

7. Proverbs 22:4
   By _____ and the _____ of the LORD are
   _____, and honour, and _____.

   riches   life   humility   fear

8. Isaiah 1:19
   If ye be _____ and _____, ye shall eat the
   _____ of the _____.

   good   land   obedient   willing

9. Matthew 6:24
   No man can _____ two _____: for either he will
   hate the one, and _____ the other; or else he will
   hold to the one, and _____ the other. Ye cannot serve
   God and _____.

   despise   love   mammon   masters   serve

10. Matthew 23:12
    And _____ shall exalt himself shall be _____;
    and he that shall _____ himself shall be _____.

    abased   humble   exalted   whosoever

11. Luke 9:48
    And said unto them, _____ shall receive this child in
    my _____ receiveth me: and whosoever shall receive
    me receiveth him that sent me: for he that is least among
    _____ all, the same shall be _____.

    name   great   Whosoever   you

12. Ephesians 3:20
    Now unto him that is able to do exceeding abundantly
    above all that we _____ or _____, according to
    the _____ that _____ in us.

    think   power   ask   worketh

10

Did You Know?

(SET 2)

Here are more little-known, interesting facts from the Bible.

- The reason the Bible states in several places that people were "going up" to Jerusalem is because Jerusalem sat on a high hill. People had to climb the hill regardless of the direction from which they approached.
- Everyone spoke the same language until God scrambled the languages at the tower of Babel (Genesis 11:1–9).
- There is an altar named Ed mentioned in Joshua 22:34.
- Earrings were the only gold items Aaron used to construct the false idol, the golden calf (Exodus 32:2–4).
- Six of the false gods mentioned in the Bible are female: Anammelech of 2 Kings 17:31; Asherah (grove) of Judges 3:7 NKJV; Diana (Artemis) of Acts 19:24; Ashtoreth of 1 Kings 11:5; queen of Heaven (Ishtar) of Jeremiah 7:18; and Succothbenoth of 2 Kings 17:30.
- The book of Job was likely written before the book of Exodus, although Exodus is the Bible's second book after Genesis.
- In 2 Kings 17:4, there is a king named So.

SPECIALIZED
MULTIPLE-CHOICE TRIVIA

Next is a large array of multiple-choice trivia by topic. Give yourself
1 point for each correct answer. Record your scores for each topic
on the score card, and as always, you may repeat any or all of the
quizzes as many times as necessary.

Take your time. This is not a race, and your ability to retain this
information is greatly enhanced if you meditate on each answer.

11

Fly High

1. What cannot be tamed even though all birds can be tamed, according to James?
   A. The mind
   B. The tongue
   C. The heart
   D. The soul

2. The Holy Spirit took the form of what bird at Jesus's baptism?
   A. Raven
   B. Pigeon
   C. Dove
   D. Eagle

3. How many of each species of bird was Noah commanded to take on to the ark?
   A. 1
   B. 3
   C. 5
   D. 7

4. Who had a vision that featured a woman with eagle's wings flying to the desert?
   A. John
   B. Paul
   C. James
   D. Peter

5. What bird was supplied in abundance to feed the Israelites in the wilderness?
   A. Eagle
   B. Quail
   C. Dove
   D. Raven

6. What parable of Jesus featured greedy birds?
   A. The tares
   B. The prodigal son
   C. The sower
   D. The great supper

What's That I Hear?

1. What apostle spoke to the Pentecost crowd in a loud voice?
   A. Peter
   B. Stephen
   C. John
   D. Judas

2. Who heard a voice talking of the fall of Babylon?
   A. John
   B. Barnabas
   C. Bartholomew
   D. Bildad

3. "This is my beloved Son, in whom I am well pleased" was spoken at what important event?
   A. Paul's conversion
   B. Jesus's baptism
   C. Peter's release from jail
   D. Jesus's ascension

4. Who heard the voice of those who had been slaughtered for proclaiming God's Word?
   A. Paul
   B. Elam
   C. John
   D. Caleb

5. Who heard the voice of God after he ran away from Queen Jezebel?
   A. Elisha
   B. David
   C. Elijah
   D. Gomer

6. What boy was sleeping near the ark of the covenant when he heard the voice of God?
   A. David
   B. Obededom
   C. Amaziah
   D. Samuel

7. What trees are broken by the power of God's voice, according to the book of Psalms?

   A. Sycamore trees
   B. Fig trees
   C. Cedars of Lebanon
   D. Lilies of the field

8. Whom did Isaiah tell that the king of Assyria had raised his voice up against God?

   A. Zechariah
   B. Hophni
   C. Zebediah
   D. Hezekiah

9. Who cried out upon seeing a vision of Samuel?

   A. Samuel's mother, Hannah
   B. Elkanah
   C. The witch of Endor
   D. King Saul

The Story of Joseph

1. How many of Joseph's brothers traveled to Egypt to buy grain?
   A. 12
   B. 10
   C. 11
   D. 6

2. Which brother of Joseph did not go down to buy grain in Egypt?
   A. Reuben
   B. Benjamin
   C. Levi
   D. Judah

3. How many days did Joseph keep his brothers in prison?
   A. 3
   B. 14
   C. 20
   D. 1

4. Which of Joseph's brothers did Joseph keep tied up until Benjamin was brought back?
   A. Reuben
   B. Manasseh
   C. Levi
   D. Simeon

5. What did Joseph command to be placed in his brothers' sacks along with grain?
   A. Money
   B. Manna
   C. Quails
   D. Sword

6. When Joseph's brothers returned, what did Joseph command to be placed in Benjamin's sack?
   A. Golden candlestick
   B. Silver cup
   C. Bronze caver
   D. Golden ring

7. What did Joseph say the man who was found in possession of the silver cup would become?
   A. His successor
   B. His friend
   C. His servant
   D. His betrayer

8. During the seven years of famine, Joseph let his father and brothers dwell in what land?
   A. Hushim
   B. Goshen
   C. Beulah
   D. Moab

9. What did Pharaoh tell Joseph that his father and his household should eat?
   A. Milk and honeycomb
   B. From the fat of the land
   C. Manna
   D. Whatever they could find

10. How old was Joseph when he died?
   A. 99 years old
   B. 100 years old
   C. 110 years old
   D. 120 years old

11. What did Joseph name his first son?
   A. Jacob
   B. Ephraim
   C. Benjamin
   D. Manasseh

12. How many pieces of silver did Joseph give to his brother Benjamin?
   A. 100
   B. 1,000
   C. 300
   D. 3,000

Have a Laugh

1. Who was laughed at for saying that a dead girl was only asleep?
   A. Paul
   B. Jesus
   C. Peter
   D. Jairus

2. What elderly man laughed at God's promise that he would father a child in his old age?
   A. Noah
   B. Methuselah
   C. Abraham
   D. Saul

3. Who danced with great enthusiasm when the ark of the covenant was brought to Jerusalem?
   A. David
   B. Solomon
   C. Obed
   D. Uzziah

4. Who laughed when told that she would bear a son in her old age?
   A. Rebekah
   B. Anna
   C. Leah
   D. Sarah

5. After the exodus, the Israelites danced in front of what graven image?
   A. A molten calf
   B. Baal
   C. A dual-horned unicorn
   D. The Semel carved image

6. What elderly woman said, "God hath made me to laugh, so that all that hear will laugh with me"?
   A. Eve
   B. Rebekah
   C. Leah
   D. Sarah

7. In the Beatitudes, to whom did Jesus promise laughter?
   A. Those who mourn
   B. Those who are sad
   C. Those who weep
   D. Those who hunger

8. Whose daughter danced after his victory over the Ammonites?
   A. Jacob's
   B. Job's
   C. Jochebed's
   D. Jephthah's

9. Who was preoccupied with dancing when David caught them?
   A. Moabites
   B. Canaanites
   C. Amalekites
   D. Philistines

10. Who laughed when he learned of Nehemiah's plans to rebuild Jerusalem?
    A. Sanballat
    B. Eliashib
    C. Shallum
    D. Benaiah

Anything Goes

1. To whom did Jesus say, "It is written again, Thou shalt not tempt the Lord thy God"?
   A. Peter
   B. Judas
   C. The devil
   D. Michael

2. When Joseph, the earthly father of Jesus, took the infant and Mary into the night, where did they go?
   A. Jerusalem
   B. Bethlehem
   C. Nazareth
   D. Egypt

3. When Jesus went into Peter's house, what was Peter's mother-in-law sick with?
   A. Leprosy
   B. Paralysis
   C. A fever
   D. An issuance of blood

4. Who was a personal servant to Moses?
   A. Caleb
   B. Joshua
   C. Aaron
   D. Jethro

5. What book of the Bible explains that a virtuous woman is more valuable than rubies?
   A. Ecclesiastes
   B. Job
   C. Psalms
   D. Proverbs

6. What crime was Jesus charged with by the high priest?
   A. Murder
   B. Blasphemy
   C. Thievery
   D. Adultery

7. Who was rewarded with the ring from King Ahasuerus of Persia?
   A. Mordecai
   B. Zeresh
   C. Adalia
   D. Esther

8. Who was David's oldest brother?
   A. Eli
   B. Adonijah
   C. Eliab
   D. Amaziah

9. Who risked her life to keep her royal nephew alive?
   A. Jehosheba
   B. Jochebed
   C. Deborah
   D. Dorcas

10. Who called herself Marah, which means "bitter"?
    A. Naomi
    B. Martha
    C. Lois
    D. Ruth

11. What apostle was exiled to the island of Patmos?
    A. Peter
    B. John
    C. James
    D. Andrew

12. What was the profession of Paul, Aquila, and Priscilla?
    A. Fishing
    B. Farming
    C. Shepherding
    D. Tentmaking

13. What prophet was thrown overboard during a powerful storm?
    A. Peter
    B. Jonah
    C. Paul
    D. Isaiah

14. Who had a daughter named Jemima?
    A. Moses
    B. Hosea
    C. Job
    D. Noah

15. Persecuted Christians were scattered throughout Judea and Samaria after the death of what person?
    A. John the Baptist
    B. Herod
    C. Stephen
    D. Judas

16. What two tribes of Israel were both descended from an Egyptian woman?
    A. Benjamin and Judah
    B. Manasseh and Ephraim
    C. Dan and Naphtali
    D. Reuben and Simeon

17. What king of Israel had a vast amount of his territory taken away by an Assyrian king?
    A. Ahab
    B. Jehoash
    C. Pekah
    D. Jehu

18. What did Jesus put on the eyes of the blind man at the pool of Siloam?
    A. Water
    B. Clay
    C. Speck
    D. Mote

19. What father of a dozen sons became blind in his old age?
    A. Jacob
    B. Isaac
    C. Abraham
    D. Job

20. What blind man of Jericho was healed by Jesus?
    A. Zacchaeus
    B. Elymas
    C. Barsabas
    D. Bartimaeus

21. What king repented after hearing the preaching of Jonah?
    A. The king of Persia
    B. The king of Nineveh
    C. The king of Syria
    D. The king of Assyria

22. What great Greek teacher who taught in the synagogue at Ephesus was himself taught by Aquila and Priscilla?
    A. Gamaliel
    B. Paul
    C. Apollos
    D. Peter

23. Whose Passover decree was laughed at by the men of Israel?
    A. Isaiah
    B. Saul
    C. Hezekiah
    D. David

24. Who rebuilt Ramah in order to keep people from coming and going to Judah?
    A. Baasha
    B. Nehemiah
    C. Jeroboam I
    D. Joram

25. What king of Judah reigned for only two years before being murdered by his own court officials?
    A. Zimri
    B. Amon
    C. Baasha
    D. Shallum

26. Who hid in a cave to escape Saul's wrath?
    A. David
    B. Solomon
    C. Jonathan
    D. Samuel

27. Who was reluctant to have Jesus wash his feet?
    A. Paul
    B. John
    C. James
    D. Peter

28. What brother of Jesus was called an apostle by Paul?

    A. John
    B. James
    C. Andrew
    D. Philip

29. Who infamously crafted a false idol, a golden calf?

    A. Moses
    B. Aaron
    C. Elijah
    D. Esau

30. Which of Saul's grandsons had crippling infirmities in his feet?

    A. Samuel
    B. Jonathan
    C. Kish
    D. Mephibosheth

31. The victory over Samaria of what Syrian king caused a famine so great that Samaritans had to survive through cannibalism?

    A. Benhadad
    B. Menahem
    C. Joash
    D. Amaziah

32. What elderly woman recognized that the baby Jesus was the Messiah?

    A. Priscilla
    B. Salome
    C. Anna
    D. Drusilla

33. Who asked Jesus for the type of water that would quench her thirst forever?

    A. The crippled woman
    B. Mary Magdalene
    C. The Samaritan woman
    D. Martha

34. Who pretended to be her husband's sister while in Egypt?

    A. Lot's wife
    B. Abram's wife, Sarai
    C. Jochebed
    D. Joseph's sister

35. What king's claim to fame was an enormous iron bed?

    A. Og
    B. Goliath
    C. Baasha
    D. Shallum

36. Who was cursed to be Israel's servants during the time of Joshua?
    A. Amorites
    B. Hittites
    C. Levites
    D. Hivites

37. Who masquerades as an angel of light, according to Paul?
    A. Michael
    B. Elymas
    C. Satan
    D. The witch of Endor

38. What king commanded that Ahimelech and some other priests be executed because they had plotted with David?
    A. Zimri
    B. Joram
    C. Pekah
    D. Saul

39. What woman ran from the empty tomb of Jesus to tell the disciples?
    A. Joanna
    B. Mary Magdalene
    C. Salome
    D. Martha

40. What king vowed loyalty to David while trying his best to kill him at the same time?
    A. Samuel
    B. Solomon
    C. Jeroboam I
    D. Saul

41. What prophet condemned those who stockpiled stolen goods?
    A. Isaiah
    B. Habakkuk
    C. Micah
    D. Jonah

42. In what parable are the servants of a landowner assaulted?
    A. The tares
    B. The hidden treasure
    C. The lost coin
    D. The wicked husbandmen

43. What king of Judah married the daughter of the sinful Ahab?
    A. Zimri
    B. Pekah
    C. Jehoram
    D. Solomon

44. In what parable are servants supplied with money to invest?
    A. The sower
    B. The talents
    C. The creditor and two debtors
    D. The minas

45. What harlot was saved from a burning city, and her family with her?
    A. Jezebel
    B. Bathsheba
    C. The witch of Endor
    D. Rahab

46. Who was in exile three years after he had his brother Amnon killed?
    A. Elijah
    B. Absalom
    C. David
    D. Achish

47. What king of Judah became king at age seven and was helped greatly by priest Jehoiada?
    A. Jehoash
    B. Joram
    C. Josiah
    D. Hoshea

48. Who had a vision in which one angel ran to meet another?
    A. Isaiah
    B. Seraiah
    C. Zechariah
    D. Balaam

49. What king of Moab was known for being a farmer of sheep?
    A. Ahaziah
    B. Jeroboam II
    C. Solomon
    D. Mesha

50. How many books comprise the New Testament?
    A. 22
    B. 25
    C. 27
    D. 33

Priests

1. What severe penalty was handed out in Israel for disobeying a priest?
   A. Imprisonment
   B. Daily confession for a year
   C. Death
   D. Daily offering of a badger for a year

2. What was etched on the twelve stones in the high priest's breastplate?
   A. The names of the kings of Israel
   B. The names of the tribes of Israel
   C. Elohim
   D. Yahweh

3. What priest was said to have had no mother or father?
   A. Ezekiel
   B. Melchisedec
   C. Joshua
   D. Ananias

4. What priest was called "King of peace"?
   A. Zacharias
   B. Melchisedec
   C. Zadok
   D. Ezra

5. What priest chastised a woman because he thought she had been drinking at the tabernacle?
   A. Eli
   B. Abiathar
   C. Joshua
   D. Phinehas

6. What king ousted all the priests who had been appointed to serve pagan gods?

   A. David

   B. Jehu

   C. Shallum

   D. Josiah

7. What greedy priest was infamous for keeping the sacrificial meat all to himself?

   A. Ahimelech

   B. Aaron

   C. Phinehas

   D. Caiaphas

8. What priest located in Midian trained Moses in how to administer justice among the Hebrews?

   A. Aaron

   B. Jethro

   C. Aleazar

   D. Eli

17

Lions' Den

1. Who saw a creature resembling a lion near the throne of God?
   A. Moses
   B. Jonathan
   C. John
   D. Samuel

2. Who envisioned a lion with eagle's wings?
   A. Jeremiah
   B. Amos
   C. Haggai
   D. Daniel

3. Who claimed to have grabbed a lion by the throat and pummeled him to death?
   A. King Hiram
   B. King Nebuchadnezzar
   C. King David
   D. King Zimri

4. What person is like a ravenous lion, according to 1 Peter?
   A. The devil
   B. Judas
   C. Herod
   D. Elymas

5. Who ripped a lion apart with his bare hands?
   A. Joshua
   B. Samson
   C. Jacob
   D. Ethan

6. What two men did David say were stronger than lions?
   A. Jacob and Joseph
   B. Saul and Jonathan
   C. Noah and Ham
   D. Abraham and Isaac

7. What prophet had a
   vision of a creature with
   a lion's face as one of its
   four sides?
   A. Isaiah
   B. Jeremiah
   C. Ezekiel
   D. Micah

8. What soldier in David's
   army killed a lion in a
   pit on a snowy day?
   A. Joab
   B. Uriah
   C. Shimei
   D. Benaiah

18

More of Anything Goes

1. Who had to shave their entire bodies as a form of consecration?
   A. Amorites
   B. Levites
   C. Philistines
   D. Gibeonites

2. A soldier of Gideon dreamed that a Midianite tent was overturned by what strange object?
   A. A grain of salt
   B. A quail from heaven
   C. A jug of milk
   D. A cake of barley bread

3. What king of Gerar took Sarah away from Abraham?
   A. Abimelech
   B. Saul
   C. Baasha
   D. Pekah

4. What wicked queen of Israel practiced witchcraft?
   A. Bathsheba
   B. Jezebel
   C. Potiphar's wife
   D. Esther

5. What leper of Bethany entertained Jesus in his home?
   A. Simeon
   B. Naaman
   C. Nadab
   D. Simon

6. What king is the author of the Song of Songs?
   A. David
   B. Solomon
   C. Moses
   D. Ahaziah

7. What king was referred to as "the Mede"?
   A. Darius
   B. Nebuchadnezzar
   C. Arioch
   D. Belshazzar

8. In the book of Ezekiel, what woman was a symbol of wicked Jerusalem?
   A. Delilah
   B. Aholibah
   C. Kezia
   D. Athaliah

9. What king sent an exiled priest back to Samaria to teach the Gentiles the proper way to follow God?
   A. The king of Assyria
   B. The king of Persia
   C. The king of Israel
   D. The king of Judah

10. What disciple outran Peter to the tomb of Jesus?
    A. John
    B. Philip
    C. Bartholomew
    D. Andrew

11. Whom did God tell to name his son Mahershalalhashbaz?
    A. Jeremiah
    B. Hosea
    C. Isaiah
    D. Iddo

12. What king of Israel was murdered while drunk?
    A. Zimri
    B. Elah
    C. Nadab
    D. Shallum

13. Who asked her son to give his father's concubine to another son?
    A. Manoah
    B. Bathsheba
    C. Deborah
    D. Rahab

14. What tribe got their wives from among the dancers at Shiloh?
    A. Dan
    B. Benjamin
    C. Naphtali
    D. Zebulun

15. Who told Job that God would fill a righteous man with laughter?
    A. Eliphaz
    B. Zophar
    C. Bildad
    D. Elihu

16. What king attacked the Israelites on their way into Canaan but was annihilated later?
    A. King Arad the Caananite
    B. King Saul
    C. The king of Syria
    D. King Joram

17. Who had a vision of a point in time when the Lord would collect the kings of the earth and put them in a pit?
    A. Jeremiah
    B. Amos
    C. Isaiah
    D. Joshua

18. What woman helped the poor in the early church?
    A. Bernice
    B. Dorcas (Tabitha)
    C. Candace
    D. Priscilla

19. The Israelites paused in their journey to the Promised Land because what woman was absent?
    A. Miriam
    B. Esther
    C. Ruth
    D. Huldah

20. Who was the last female to have dinner with King Saul?
    A. The witch of Endor
    B. Ahinoam
    C. The woman of Tekoa
    D. Merab

21. Whom did the prophet Elijah miraculously supply with food?
    A. Jezebel
    B. The widow of Zarephath
    C. Jerioth
    D. The Shulamite woman

22. What woman did Elisha warn of an approaching famine?
    A. The woman of Tishbite
    B. Ahab's wife
    C. The woman of Shunem
    D. Maachah

23. How was the adulterous woman going to be punished before she was forgiven by Jesus?
    A. Crucifixion
    B. Stoning
    C. Starvation
    D. Prison

24. In what book are the sons of God described as taking the daughters of men as wives?
    A. Genesis
    B. Exodus
    C. Leviticus
    D. Numbers

25. Where did Mary and Martha live?
    A. Samaria
    B. Bethany
    C. Jerusalem
    D. Jericho

26. There was a plot hatched against Jesus in the home of what person?
    A. Ananias
    B. Phinehas
    C. Zacharias
    D. Caiaphas

27. All the priests of Israel originated from what tribe?
    A. Judah
    B. Benjamin
    C. Levi
    D. Joseph

28. Who was the first metal worker named in the Bible?
    A. Abel
    B. Seth
    C. Noah
    D. Tubalcain

29. After Eve, who was the second woman mentioned in the Bible?
    A. Abel's wife
    B. Enoch's wife
    C. Cain's wife
    D. Adah

30. God made his first covenant with Noah and his second covenant with whom?
    A. Adam
    B. Abraham
    C. Cain
    D. Lamech

31. What was the second recorded miracle of Jesus?
    A. The raising of Lazarus
    B. Healing the man born blind
    C. Walking on the sea
    D. Healing an official's son in Cana

32. Paul first traveled with Barnabas before traveling with whom?
    A. Peter
    B. Silas
    C. Timothy
    D. John Mark

33. Who was Jacob's second son?
    A. Simeon
    B. Joseph
    C. Benjamin
    D. Dan

34. Who followed Saul as king of Israel?
    A. Samuel
    B. David
    C. Ishbosheth
    D. Jeroboam I

35. Who lived for 962 years?

A. Seth

B. Jared

C. Mahalalel

D. Lamech

36. After Solomon built the first temple in Jerusalem, who built the second?

A. Joshua and Caleb

B. Rehoboam and Jeroboam

C. Asa and Abijam

D. Zerubbabel and Jeshua

37. Who heard the voice of God speaking out of a whirlwind?

A. Elisha

B. Nathan

C. Paul

D. Job

38. Who was permanently crippled due to a servant woman dropping him as a baby?

A. Balaam

B. Saul's brother

C. Mephibosheth

D. Jonathan's grandson

39. Who committed suicide by hanging because Absalom would not follow his advice?

A. Ahithophel

B. Amnon

C. Hushai

D. Joab

40. What warrior wore a coat of mail weighing over 5,000 shekels of brass (over 125 pounds)?

A. Goliath

B. Samson

C. David

D. Methuselah

41. What did Malachi say the people of Judah were stealing from God?
    A. Idols
    B. Taxes
    C. Tithes and offerings
    D. Lands

42. When Jerusalem fell to the hands of the Babylonians, who was the king?
    A. Hezekiah
    B. Nebuchadnezzar
    C. Jeroboam II
    D. Zedekiah

43. What priest led a revolt in Judah that resulted in people tearing down their Baal temple and destroying idols?
    A. Jehoiada
    B. Asa
    C. Josiah
    D. Ahab

44. What priest dedicated the newly rebuilt walls of Jerusalem?
    A. Eleazar
    B. Pashur
    C. Zadok
    D. Eliashib

45. Who spoke the words of Joel in a sermon?
    A. John
    B. Paul
    C. Peter
    D. Thomas

46. What woman did Paul commend for her hard work?
    A. Phebe
    B. Mary
    C. Sapphira
    D. Susanna

47. Who was able to entice Herod to the point that he offered her anything she wanted?
    A. The daughter of Caiaphas
    B. Tabitha
    C. The daughter of Herodias
    D. Damaris

48. Who was told by
    God to name his son
    Loammi?
    A. Micah
    B. Amos
    C. Joel
    D. Hosea

49. What son of David tried
    to make himself king of
    Israel?
    A. Jesse
    B. Adonijah
    C. Solomon
    D. Abner

50. What Canaanite king
    had nine hundred
    chariots of iron?
    A. Hezekiah
    B. Jabin
    C. Ahaziah
    D. Pekah

51. Who was the only
    Egyptian queen
    mentioned in the Bible?
    A. Tahpenes
    B. Esther
    C. The queen of Sheba
    D. Candace

52. What was the affliction
    of the ten men who
    cried out to Jesus,
    begging him for mercy?
    A. Blindness
    B. Deafness
    C. Leprosy
    D. Paralysis

53. What miracle of Jesus
    prompted the priests
    to plot to have him
    executed?
    A. The temple tax in
       the fish's mouth
    B. The escape from the
       hostile multitude
    C. The raising of
       Lazarus from the
       dead
    D. The healing of a
       centurion's servant

54. What rotund king of
    Moab was murdered by
    the judge Ehud?
    A. Zimri
    B. Solomon
    C. Eglon
    D. David

55. What woman had already had five husbands and was living with another man?
   A. Martha
   B. The woman with the issue of blood
   C. Mary Magdalene
   D. The Samaritan woman

56. What woman made her living selling purple cloth?
   A. Priscilla
   B. Claudia
   C. Lydia
   D. Lois

57. What church had a sexually immoral woman named Jezebel?
   A. Ephesus
   B. Smyrna
   C. Pergamos
   D. Thyatira

58. What king's wife disguised herself in order to seek counsel with the prophet Ahijah?
   A. Potiphar's
   B. Jeroboam's
   C. David's
   D. Job's

59. What two apostles were imprisoned in Jerusalem for preaching the gospel?
   A. Paul and Barnabas
   B. Peter and John
   C. Titus and Timothy
   D. Paul and Timothy

60. Who had a dream in which God warned that Jacob should not be pursued or harmed?
   A. Laban
   B. Leah
   C. Nahor
   D. Bethuel

61. What king introduced Israel to the worship of the false god Baal?
    A. Elijah
    B. Ahab
    C. Jehoshaphat
    D. Shallum

62. What king established a beauty contest in order to select a bride?
    A. Ahasuerus
    B. Malcham
    C. Joahaz
    D. Nethaniah

63. Who prophesied the destruction of Jerusalem?
    A. Peter
    B. Thomas
    C. Herod
    D. Jesus

64. Who built an altar unto the Lord and called it Jehovahnissi?
    A. Abraham
    B. Noah
    C. Moses
    D. Aaron

65. What prophet foresaw the destruction of the altars of Bethel?
    A. Nahum
    B. Joel
    C. Habakkuk
    D. Amos

66. Who murdered Shallum and replaced him on the throne of Israel?
    A. Shamar
    B. Menahem
    C. Baasha
    D. Jehoash

67. Whom did the Sanhedrin jail for disturbing the peace?
    A. Paul and Barnabas
    B. Timothy and Titus
    C. Peter and John
    D. Stephen and Silas

68. Who preached to the intellectual elite of Athens?
    A. Paul
    B. Peter
    C. Jesus
    D. Gamaliel

69. After Sodom and Gomorrah were destroyed, who gathered his daughters and lived in a cave?
   A. Abraham
   B. Caleb
   C. Elijah
   D. Lot

70. What is the fortieth book of the Bible?
   A. Haggai
   B. Malachi
   C. Luke
   D. Matthew

19

Did You Know?

(SET 3)

Ready for more astonishing facts? Help yourself.

- In the early thirteenth century, Archbishop Stephen Langton developed a system for dividing the Bible into chapters.
- At the grand dedication of God's temple, Solomon had 22,000 oxen and 120,000 sheep sacrificed (1 Kings 8:62–63).
- After the Israelites destroyed the temple of Baal, they used it as a communal latrine (draught house) (2 Kings 10:26–27).
- Luke, the only physician among the disciples, chronicled that as Jesus was praying in the Garden of Gethsemane before he was crucified, his extreme duress caused his perspiration to become like large drops of blood falling to the ground. This phenomenon is a medical condition called hematidrosis that only Luke the physician documented.
- Although dogs are mentioned in the Bible forty-one times, cats are not mentioned at all.
- God himself buried Moses in Moab, but no one knows precisely where (Deuteronomy 34:5–6).
- In Joshua 3:16, there is a town called Adam.

SCRIPTURE FILL IN THE BLANKS

Fill in the blanks to complete the following Scripture passages.
Give yourself 2 points for each correct passage.

20

Scriptures on Hope

1. Numbers 23:19

   God is not a _____, that he should _____;
   neither the son of man, that he should repent: hath he
   said, and shall he not do it? or hath he spoken, and shall
   he not make it _____?

2. Job 13:15

   Though he _____ me, yet will I _____ in him:
   but I will maintain mine own _____ before him.

3. Proverbs 24:14

   So shall the knowledge of _____ be unto thy
   _____: when thou hast found it, then there shall be a
   reward, and thy _____ shall not be cut off.

4. Proverbs 24:20

   For there shall be no reward to the _____ man; the
   candle of the _____ shall be put out.

5. Romans 8:24–25

   For we are saved by _____: but hope that is seen is
   not _____: for what a man seeth, why doth he yet
   hope for? But if we hope for that we see not, then do we
   with _____ wait for it.

6. 1 Corinthians 15:19

   If in this _____ only we have hope in _____, we
   are of all men most _____.

7. Hebrews 11:1

Now _____ is the substance of things _____ for, the evidence of _____ not seen.

8. 1 Peter 1:3

Blessed be the _____ and Father of our Lord Jesus _____, which according to his abundant mercy hath begotten us again unto a lively hope by the _____ of Jesus Christ from the _____.

Scriptures on Love

1. Leviticus 19:17–18

   Thou shalt not hate thy _____ in thine heart: thou shalt in any wise rebuke thy neighbour, and not suffer _____ upon him. Thou shalt not avenge, nor bear any grudge against the _____ of thy people, but thou shalt _____ thy neighbour as thyself: I am the LORD.

2. Psalm 30:5

   For his _____ endureth but a moment; in his favour is _____: weeping may endure for a _____, but joy cometh in the morning.

3. Psalm 103:8

   The _____ is merciful and _____, slow to anger, and plenteous in _____.

4. Psalm 103:13

   Like as a _____ pitieth his _____, so the LORD pitieth them that fear _____.

5. Psalm 143:8

   Cause me to hear thy lovingkindness in the _____; for in thee do I trust: cause me to know the way wherein I should _____; for I lift up my soul unto thee.

6. Proverbs 10:12

   _____ stirreth up strifes: but _____ covereth all sins.

7. Proverbs 21:21

   He that followeth after _____ and mercy findeth _____, righteousness, and honour.

8. Isaiah 43:4

   Since thou wast precious in my _____, thou hast been honourable, and I have loved _____: therefore will I give _____ for thee, and people for thy _____.

9. Matthew 5:44

   But I say unto you, _____ your _____, bless them that curse you, do good to them that hate you, and pray for them which despitefully use you, and persecute _____.

10. Mark 12:30

    And thou shalt _____ the Lord thy God with all thy _____, and with all thy soul, and with all thy mind, and with all thy strength: this is the first _____.

11. Mark 12:31

    And the second is like, namely this, Thou shalt _____ thy neighbour as thyself. There is none other _____ greater than these.

12. Luke 10:27

    And he answering said, _____ shalt love the Lord thy God with all thy _____, and with all thy _____, and with all thy strength, and with all thy mind; and thy neighbour as thyself.

13. John 14:21

    He that hath my _____, and keepeth them, he it is that _____ me: and he that loveth me shall be loved of my _____, and I will love him, and will manifest myself to him.

14. John 15:12

    This is my _____, That ye _____ one another, as
    I have _____ you.

15. John 15:13

    Greater love hath no _____ than this, that a man lay
    down his _____ for his _____.

16. Romans 8:38–39

    For I am _____, that neither death, nor life, nor
    angels, nor principalities, nor _____, nor things
    present, nor things to come, nor _____, nor depth,
    nor any other creature, shall be able to separate us from
    the love of _____, which is in Christ Jesus our Lord.

17. Romans 12:9

    Let _____ be without dissimulation. Abhor that
    which is _____; cleave to that which is good.

18. Romans 12:10

    Be kindly affectioned one to another with brotherly
    _____; in honour preferring one another.

19. Romans 13:8

    Owe no man any thing, but to _____ one another:
    for he that loveth another hath fulfilled the _____.

20. Romans 13:10

    _____ worketh no _____ to his neighbour:
    therefore love is the fulfilling of the law.

21. 1 Corinthians 2:9

    But as it is _____, Eye hath not seen, nor ear
    _____, neither have entered into the heart of man,
    the things which God hath prepared for them that
    _____ him.

22. 1 Corinthians 10:24
    Let no _____ seek his own, but every man another's
    _____.

23. 1 Corinthians 13:1
    Though I speak with the _____ of men and of
    _____, and have not charity, I am become as
    sounding brass, or a tinkling _____.

24. 1 Corinthians 13:2
    And though I have the gift of _____, and understand
    all _____, and all knowledge; and though I have all
    faith, so that I could remove _____, and have not
    charity, I am nothing.

25. 1 Corinthians 13:3
    And though I bestow all my _____ to feed the poor,
    and though I give my _____ to be burned, and have
    not charity, it profiteth me _____.

26. 1 Corinthians 13:4–5
    _____ suffereth long, and is kind; charity envieth
    not; charity vaunteth not itself, is not puffed up, doth not
    _____ itself unseemly, seeketh not her own, is not
    easily provoked, thinketh no _____.

27. 1 Corinthians 16:14
    Let all your _____ be done with _____.

28. Ephesians 3:16–17
    That he would grant you, according to the _____
    of his _____, to be strengthened with might by his
    _____ in the inner man; that Christ may dwell in
    your hearts by faith; that ye, being rooted and grounded
    in _____.

29. Ephesians 4:2
    With all lowliness and _____, with longsuffering,
    forbearing one another in _____.

30. Ephesians 4:15
    But speaking the truth in _____, may grow up into
    him in all _____, which is the head, even _____.

31. Ephesians 5:2
    And walk in love, as Christ also hath _____ us, and
    hath given _____ for us an offering and a sacrifice to
    _____ for a sweetsmelling savour.

32. Ephesians 5:25–26
    _____, love your _____, even as Christ also
    loved the church, and gave himself for it; That he might
    sanctify and cleanse it with the washing of water by the
    word.

33. Colossians 3:14
    And above all these things put on _____, which is the
    bond of _____.

34. 1 Thessalonians 3:12
    And the Lord make you to increase and abound in
    _____ one toward another, and toward all _____,
    even as we do toward you.

35. 2 Thessalonians 3:5
    And the Lord direct your _____ into the love of God,
    and into the _____ waiting for Christ.

36. 2 Timothy 1:7
    For God hath not given us the spirit of _____; but of
    power, and of love, and of a sound _____.

37. 1 Peter 4:8

    And above all things have fervent _____ among
    yourselves: for charity shall cover the multitude of
    _____.

38. 1 John 3:1

    Behold, what manner of love the _____ hath
    bestowed upon _____, that we should be called the
    sons of God: therefore the world knoweth us not, because
    it knew him not.

39. 1 John 3:11

    For this is the message that ye heard from the _____,
    that we should _____ one another.

40. 1 John 4:9

    In this was manifested the _____ of God toward us,
    because that God sent his only begotten Son into the
    _____, that we might live through him.

41. 1 John 4:10

    Herein is _____, not that we loved God, but that he
    loved us, and sent his _____ to be the propitiation for
    our _____.

42. 1 John 4:12

    No man hath seen _____ at any time. If we love one
    another, God dwelleth in us, and his love is perfected in
    _____.

43. 1 John 4:16

    And we have known and believed the _____ that God
    hath to us. God is _____; and he that dwelleth in love
    dwelleth in God, and God in him.

44. 1 John 4:18
    There is no fear in love; but perfect _____ casteth out
    _____: because fear hath torment. He that feareth is
    not made perfect in _____.

45. 1 John 4:20
    If a man say, I love God, and hateth his brother, he is a
    _____: for he that loveth not his _____ whom he
    hath seen, how can he love God whom he hath not seen?

46. Revelation 3:19
    As many as I _____, I rebuke and _____: be
    zealous therefore, and repent.

SECTION 2

THE ADVANCED SECTION

This section gets into very specific and challenging questions and puzzles geared to take you to an extreme level of Bible brilliance. (Answers to section 2 begin on page 221.)

If we abide by the principles taught in the Bible, our country will go on prospering but if we and our posterity neglect its instructions and authority, no man can tell how sudden a catastrophe may overwhelm us and bury all our glory in profound obscurity.

Daniel Webster, American statesman and the
fourteenth United States secretary of state

SPECIALIZED
TRUE OR FALSE TRIVIA

For 1 point per correct answer, tackle this section of true or false statements derived from all areas of the Bible. Some are easy, and some are quite difficult. Do one group at a time and record your score for each group on the score card.

Remember, you may do a single group as many times as necessary before posting your best score. It is far more important to be thorough and to learn this information than to finish quickly and retain little.

Group 1

1. _____ The woman at the well had at least five husbands.

2. _____ Jesus asked the woman at the well for bread to eat.

3. _____ In the Gospel of John, the Sea of Galilee is called the Sea of Tiberias.

4. _____ Peter betrayed Jesus with a kiss.

5. _____ Satan is the father of lies.

6. _____ Peter asked his shipmates to cast him into the sea.

7. _____ Jonah was in the belly of a great fish for four days and four nights.

8. _____ In an attempt to run from the presence of the Lord, Jonah tried to flee to Tarshish.

9. _____ Jonah danced while inside a giant fish.

10. _____ Jonah proclaimed that Nineveh would be overturned in sixty days.

11. _____ Nun was Joshua's brother.

12. _____ The Euphrates is described as "the great river" in the book of Joshua.

13. _____ Joshua sent spies into Jericho.

14. _____ Joshua was 120 years old when he died.

15. _____ Joseph's bones were buried at Shechem.

16. _____ Levi was the first tribe to enter the Promised Land.

17. _____ The city of Jericho was famous for its fallen walls.

18. _____ Jephthah ran from his brothers and dwelt in the land of Tob.

19. _____ Abdon had fifty-two sons.

20. _____ Elimelech was Samson's father.

23

Group 2

1. _____ Samson ate honey from the carcass of a lion he killed.

2. _____ Samson lost his power when his hair was cut off.

3. _____ Elisha was buried with his father, Manoah.

4. _____ Achan stole eleven hundred pieces of silver from his mother.

5. _____ Micah made his son a priest over all his idols.

6. _____ Eglon, the king of Moab, was a very skinny man.

7. _____ King Eglon was slain by Ehud.

8. _____ Jael gave a captain wine and then killed him.

9. _____ Jabin was the king of the Philistines.

10. _____ Nebuchadnezzar was killed by Jael as he slept in a tent.

11. _____ Israel was once judged by the prophetess Ruth.

12. _____ Moses was commissioned by an angel to save Israel from the Midianites.

13. _____ Gideon and his men attacked Israelite soldiers late at night.

14. _____ The Midianite Zeeb was murdered at his winepress by David's army.

15. _____ Gideon defeated the Midianites with only 350
    men.

16. _____ The Midianites had gold chains around the necks
    of their camels.

17. _____ During the time of Gideon, the Israelites
    experienced forty years of turmoil.

18. _____ Gideon had seventy sons.

19. _____ Goats were forbidden as food to the Israelites.

20. _____ The law instructed lepers to cover their hair at all
    times.

24

Group 3

1. _____ A ram was released into the wilderness bearing the sins of Israel.

2. _____ Moses anointed Aaron and his daughters with the blood of a ram.

3. _____ Nadab and Abihu were the sons of Moses.

4. _____ While in the temple of God, Zacharias lost his voice.

5. _____ Mary was married when Jesus was born.

6. _____ Mary was told by the angel Gabriel that her son was to be named Jesus.

7. _____ Jesus saw Satan falling as lightning from heaven.

8. _____ The eyes are called the lamp of the body.

9. _____ A singing Christian causes angels to rejoice, according to Jesus.

10. _____ On a single occasion, Jesus healed ten lepers.

11. _____ When Jesus healed ten lepers, only one returned to thank him.

12. _____ Zacchaeus climbed a tree so he could see Jesus.

13. _____ Zacchaeus gave half of his wealth to the poor.

14. _____ Anna and Simeon saw Jesus in the manger.

15. _____ The city of David was Bethlehem.

16. _____ Jesus's parents went to Jerusalem every year for the feast of the Passover.

17. _____ When Jesus was twelve, he referred to the temple in Jerusalem as his Father's house.

18. _____ Jesus's hometown was Nazareth.

19. _____ Jesus was born in a small, cramped cottage.

20. _____ The Lord's Supper was to be a reminder of Christ's body and blood.

Group 4

1. _____ An angel came to strengthen Jesus when he was in Gethsemane.

2. _____ While Jesus prayed in Gethsemane, the disciples were sleeping.

3. _____ Jesus frequently went to the Mount of Olives.

4. _____ After his resurrection, Jesus had his first dinner in the village of Emmaus.

5. _____ Pontius Pilate was a tax collector.

6. _____ A garner is a place to store grain.

7. _____ The tax collector Matthew held a feast for Jesus.

8. _____ Matthew was also known as Levi.

9. _____ Peter said to Jesus, "Depart from me; for I am a sinful man, O Lord."

10. _____ Jesus told his disciples to pray for the people who curse them.

11. _____ Jesus brought the dead son of the widow of Nain back to life.

12. _____ Paul was asleep on a boat during a storm on the Sea of Galilee.

13. _____ Jesus brought Jairus's wife back to life.

14. _____ Jesus sent James and Andrew to prepare the Passover meal.

15. _____ At Jesus's baptism, the Holy Spirit took the form of a swan.

16. _____ John the Baptist baptized people in the Nile River.

17. _____ Moses said he was unworthy to unloosen another man's sandals.

18. _____ Jesus accused the Pharisees of devouring widows' houses.

19. _____ Simon the leper entertained Jesus in his home.

20. _____ The word *Golgotha* is translated "the place of a skull."

26

Group 5

1. _____ Three criminals were crucified with Jesus.

2. _____ Jesus told his followers that they would have the power to safely handle dangerous snakes.

3. _____ Serpents were cast out of Mary Magdalene.

4. _____ Mary Magdalene was healed by Jesus of seven demons.

5. _____ James and John were "the sons of thunder."

6. _____ When Jesus entered a town or village, people placed the sick in the marketplaces.

7. _____ Joseph was told in a dream about the miraculous conception of Jesus.

8. _____ Emmanuel means "the anointed one."

9. _____ Jesus descended from the tribe of Judah.

10. _____ Jesus said you can recognize a tree by its fruit.

11. _____ Jesus used seven loaves of bread to feed five thousand people.

12. _____ James was enabled by Jesus to briefly walk on water.

13. _____ Herodias, the wife of Herod, plotted the death of King David.

14. _____ Jesus sent Matthew to catch a fish with a coin in its mouth.

15. _____ A map led the wise men to the baby Jesus.

16. _____ When the wise men saw a peculiar star, they were in the west.

17. _____ Jesus cursed a fig tree because it did not bear fruit.

18. _____ Matthew is the only Gospel to mention Jesus riding on a donkey.

19. _____ Jesus talked about end times from the Mount of Olives.

20. _____ Jesus delivered his final discourse on the Mount of Olives.

27

Group 6

1. _____ In the Bible, sometimes Christians are referred to as lambs.

2. _____ Judas was given fifty pieces of silver to betray Jesus.

3. _____ The chief priests paid Judas Iscariot to betray Jesus.

4. _____ Peter denied Jesus five times.

5. _____ Peter wept bitterly after denying the Lord.

6. _____ The prisoner Barabbas was released in place of Jesus.

7. _____ The criminals crucified next to Christ were murderers.

8. _____ A huge stone was used to seal the tomb that temporarily held Jesus.

9. _____ The potter's field was also known as "the field of worship."

10. _____ John the Baptist preached in the wilderness in Judea.

11. _____ John the Baptist ate locusts and honey in the wilderness.

12. _____ John the Baptist wore a tunic made of camel hair.

13. _____ After Jesus was tempted in the wilderness, God ministered to him.

14. _____ After leaving Nazareth, Jesus moved to Bethany.

15. _____ Jesus said, "Man shall not live by water alone."

16. _____ God said a foolish man builds his house on mud.

17. _____ Hosea prophesied Assyria's destruction.

18. _____ Moses wrote the first six books of the Bible.

19. _____ Hannah's story takes place in 2 Chronicles.

20. _____ The serpent was cursed by God.

28

Group 7

1. _____ Mary, the mother of Jesus, had no other children.

2. _____ Numbers is the third book of the Old Testament.

3. _____ The book of Jude comes before the book of Revelation in the New Testament.

4. _____ Ruth is the tenth book of the Old Testament.

5. _____ Luke is the shortest book of the New Testament.

6. _____ The story of Samson is found in the book of Acts.

7. _____ Levi (Matthew) was the son of Alphaeus.

8. _____ Idolatry is the worship of false gods.

9. _____ Jesus prophesied the destruction of Jerusalem.

10. _____ The story of Leah is recorded in the book of Genesis.

11. _____ The Jordan River connects the Dead Sea with the Sea of Galilee.

12. _____ James and John were the sons of Zebedee.

13. _____ Hosanna means "thank the Lord."

14. _____ There are twenty-seven books in the New Testament.

15. _____ Amos is the last book of the Old Testament.

16. _____ The first word of the Bible is "in."

17. _____ The longest chapter in the Bible is Psalm 119 with 176 verses.

18. _____ The third book of the Old Testament is Exodus.

19. _____ The fifth book of the New Testament is Romans.

20. _____ The Lord used wind from the sea to bring quail to the Israelites.

29

Group 8

1. _____ Moses sent twelve spies into Canaan.

2. _____ Because Korah and his men were rebellious, the earth swallowed them up.

3. _____ The house of Israel mourned Aaron's death for forty days.

4. _____ The prophet Balaam had a talking donkey.

5. _____ Phinehas killed two people at the same time with a single spear.

6. _____ Aaron was one hundred years old when he died.

7. _____ Aaron died on Mount Hor.

8. _____ When Paul was in Thessalonica, the Philippians sent help to him.

9. _____ Solomon compared a lovely woman who lacks discretion to a jewel of gold in a swine's snout.

10. _____ According to Proverbs, the bread of deceit is sweet to man.

11. _____ The proverbs of Solomon were copied by the men of Hezekiah, the king of Judah.

12. _____ Open rebuke is better than hidden love.

13. _____ There are sixty-six books in the Bible.

14. _____ Genesis has fifty chapters.

15. _____ Noah had a vision of Jesus walking among seven golden lampstands.

16. _____ The book of Genesis says that the divine voice sounds like a waterfall.

17. _____ The seven churches in the book of Revelation were located in Asia.

18. _____ In a vision, John was told to measure the temple in Jerusalem.

19. _____ According to Revelation, the beast will ascend out of the abyss and slay the two witnesses.

20. _____ In heaven, Michael and his angels fought against the dragon.

Group 9

1. _____ The book of Revelation mentions a talking altar.

2. _____ In Revelation, the great harlot rode on a scarlet beast.

3. _____ John heard a voice speaking of the fall of Babylon.

4. _____ In the book of Revelation, the fiery lake was composed of burning wood.

5. _____ In the book of Revelation, an angel bound Satan with a chain.

6. _____ Seven angels were at the gates of the new Jerusalem.

7. _____ The new Jerusalem was decorated with twelve precious stones.

8. _____ The church of Laodicea was neither hot nor cold.

9. _____ Moses had a vision of a sea of glass.

10. _____ Daniel saw a creature that resembled a lion near the throne of God.

11. _____ When John saw the four angels standing on the four corners of the earth, they were dancing.

12. _____ In Revelation, sand fell on earth's waters to make them bitter.

13. _____ Faith comes by hearing the Word of God.

14. _____ Jesus Christ will judge all of mankind.

15. _____ Paul said to greet one another with a holy hug.

16. _____ The apostle Paul had the book of Romans written down for him by Tertius.

17. _____ The wages of sin is death.

18. _____ Nothing can separate us from God's love.

19. _____ Joseph was Naomi's husband.

20. _____ Ruth was married to Chilion of Israel.

31

Group 10

1. _____ Ruth had a sister-in-law named Orpah.

2. _____ Ruth's first husband was Mahlon.

3. _____ One of Jesus's ancestors was a Moabite named Ruth.

4. _____ Solomon had a throne with blue cushions.

5. _____ There are twenty-nine books in the Old Testament.

6. _____ Zenas was a lawyer.

7. _____ Zechariah had a vision of an angel on a red horse.

8. _____ The book of Zechariah describes the Mount of Olives splitting in half.

9. _____ During the time of Zechariah, Saul was the high priest.

10. _____ Obadiah wrote a book against Edom.

32

Did You Know?

(SET 4)

Here are more absolutely amazing facts to ponder.

- Second Samuel 21:20 speaks of a man with twelve fingers and twelve toes.
- As Jesus was being crucified, three of the four women present were named Mary.
- The word *amen* means "so be it."
- Jerusalem at one time was called Jebus (Judges 19:10).
- Samson's incredible head of hair featured only seven separate locks (Judges 16:19).
- The apostle Paul had a sister (Acts 23:16).
- There was a man named Judas who lived on a street named Straight, or Straight Street (Acts 9:11).

WORD SEARCHES

Word searches are fun. In these puzzles, words are placed horizontally, vertically, and diagonally, both forward and backward. Some words may overlap in the puzzle. Simply circle the words in the list in whatever direction they appear. But here's the Bible brilliant twist. For the first two word searches of a topic, you will have the list of words. For the third puzzle of the series, you will not have the list of words but must still find them all.

Women in the Bible Part 1

Find the following names of women in the Bible. Give yourself 10 points if you find them all.

```
R X D I N A H E B E O H P H Q
E H A N N A H I N O A M L M B
H N B S F R M L A P L V H D R
T Q R S M I U D E B O R A H O
S I E P A D B T E B I L H A H
E J H V N R V V H O E L J T Y
Q B T K P S A C R O D Z L J R
H A E Q Q N Y H C Q B E E H J
A T B L Z R A B I G A I L J U
L H A G A R G V E H N Q H K D
I S S M Q A G P K E V L U B I
L H I G X C D A M A R I S S T
E E L H Z H Q L P D Q D K T H
D B E A Q E B R A Y H E I F X
C A R O Q L I B M O T X X C O
```

ABIGAIL (1 Samuel 25:3)
AHINOAM (1 Samuel 14:50)
BATHSHEBA (2 Samuel 12:24)
BILHAH (Genesis 29:29)
DAMARIS (Acts 17:34)
DEBORAH (Genesis 35:8)
DELILAH (Judges 16:4)
DINAH (Genesis 30:21)
DORCAS (Acts 9:36)
ELISABETH (Luke 1:7)
ESTHER (book of Esther)
HAGAR (Genesis 16:1)
HANNAH (1 Samuel 1:2)
JEZEBEL (1 Kings 16:31)
JUDITH (Genesis 26:34)
LEAH (Genesis 29:16)
MARY (Matthew 1:16)
PHOEBE (Romans 16:1 NKJV)
RACHEL (Genesis 29:6)
RUTH (book of Ruth)
SARAH (Genesis 17:15)

Women in the Bible Part 2

Once again, find the following women's names. If you find them all, give yourself 10 points.

```
K E A J H A N I D T J V Y X C
U B M W O K J W H T I D U J J
M E F A X L E H C A R A G A H
H O E L I S A B E T H Q I Y W
A H W Z I H B L J E Z E B E L
N P X A U A Z F L Y S N H A E
N O C B J H G U F Z U A S S Y
A R G E S L J I P D R I R M T
H E D H A I T O B O R U U A Q
I H E S C B E B B A T R X P H
N T L H R Y G E M H H A E L G
O S I T O U D A X M O N I W Z
A E L A D T D D V A Y U X K A
M C A B S P X U B R Z B F R L
P T H T G E M C J Y X S U N Z
```

ABIGAIL	DINAH	JUDITH
AHINOAM	DORCAS	LEAH
BATHSHEBA	ELISABETH	MARY
BILHAH	ESTHER	PHOEBE
DAMARIS	HAGAR	RACHEL
DEBORAH	HANNAH	RUTH
DELILAH	JEZEBEL	SARAH

Women in the Bible Part 3

If you find all twenty-one names, give yourself 25 points.

```
N  S  E  U  V  M  A  O  N  I  H  A  L  H  Q
D  E  B  O  R  A  H  K  F  A  M  I  F  Q  P
D  M  E  I  H  Y  D  U  N  D  A  T  D  R  N
Q  N  O  P  U  O  H  N  H  G  O  J  T  B  M
H  Z  H  I  E  G  A  K  I  H  G  R  R  Y  I
R  B  P  J  I  H  G  B  K  A  E  Y  C  M  B
A  I  X  Z  E  D  A  A  U  L  S  G  R  A  B
C  L  A  H  C  Z  R  C  I  I  T  O  W  G  S
H  H  P  N  A  U  E  S  B  L  H  E  N  Z  A
E  A  D  Q  U  N  A  B  C  E  E  O  H  F  H
L  H  E  G  L  B  I  O  E  D  R  A  C  J  T
R  O  B  L  E  D  P  D  P  L  R  Z  X  M  I
U  B  A  T  H  S  H  E  B  A  W  K  A  X  D
T  O  H  V  A  X  R  Q  S  X  C  R  U  X  U
H  W  N  S  I  R  A  M  A  D  Y  X  H  U  J
```

36

Paul's Journeys Part 1

If you find the following words concerning the travels of the apostle Paul, give yourself 10 points.

```
A I C Y L E A T H O J P L Z W
G C H M R O V Z A F Z B F C D
Q M O Y R A N R Y M S N A O X
K B T G A L A T I A K L U L P
S E G I S T A P J C D Y X O E
S U D S A W T I A L A S X S Z
E U S P U V Z I N O Y T W S P
D B U R T R N D T O G R N E X
O H O R A O P K I R L A E C S
H F O L D T P Y O S T O A G Y
R A R E K H G U C S I N P V R
S E C A R H T U H Y L Z O P I
J A Y S H H S T X T M P L M A
M K H I V I V N G Y I V I R W
B G S A L A M I S N Y U S S P
```

ANTIOCH	LYSTRA	SYRIA
APPOLONIA	MACEDONIA	TARSUS
ASIA	NEAPOLIS	THRACE
COLOSSE	PATARA	TROAS
CYPRUS	RHODES	TYRE
GALATIA	SALAMIS	
LYCIA	SMYRNA	

Paul's Journeys Part 2

Once again, find the following words related to Paul's journeys. If you find them all, give yourself 10 points.

```
K Q E F S P A T A R A A I C C
G E N X A Z M B D I I E V O S
A S I L O P A E N R O W L D A
L N M E R N J Y Y R H O D E S
A H S Y T A R S U S S Q W I R
T P O I R O S G S S V A B W J
I I O L Q N R K E U F I A B A
A C S S I M A L A S R M J K I
H K E L A I N O L O P P A Y N
E I C H H D A Y S E L G Y G O
Q Q A D C H C I R Y D U J C D
H R R O S I Z Y S O Q D Y F E
P G H E A U T T S A U I W M C
U X T K L X R E K B P S H X A
V M Q O S A C B Q H P M C S M
```

ANTIOCH	LYSTRA	SYRIA
APPOLONIA	MACEDONIA	TARSUS
ASIA	NEAPOLIS	THRACE
COLOSSE	PATARA	TROAS
CYPRUS	RHODES	TYRE
GALATIA	SALAMIS	
LYCIA	SMYRNA	

Paul's Journeys Part 3

If you find all nineteen words, give yourself 25 points.

A P P O L O N I A I R R P F X
E R U J F U L K R N S T O B O
N H K A K R A E A A R T Y R E
A O E D J I K S T C J Y V E C
N D O A C W B S A R C Q M Y Y
T E S Y S I L O P A E N M S P
I S L X L A W L N Z B E D M R
O Y U S X I S O E F G K U Y U
C R Z H M T I C S I M A L A S
H B O C S A W D Z A A K S S D
A R T S Y L S T A P S I X U J
J R V Y L A S X X L A G D S I
A E B Y D G V R E I I B T R E
S Y R I A M A C E D O N I A V
T H R A C E F T S A O R T T N

Prisoners and Exiles Part 1

Find the following names of prisoners and exiles. If you find them all, give yourself 10 points.

```
S U S M L I S A I A H D O Q P
D I U V O M A N A S S E H M E
J A U U F R Z E D E K I A H T
G O N T M S D O W V Q N D Y E
I X H I R O H E Q T S B O C R
Y K M N E P R S C R Z E Y A S
J W D Q E L J T O A C A I N H
E S Z S F O T H L Q I Z E F G
R X O Q X A X E K L Q A O E N
E J M J Q Z P R J A C O B E X
M Y Z K D A Q A Z L W Z H S R
I U W Z Q R A R U K O P C I X
A L F E G I M D J L E Z A L A
H H M M V A R Y N T H A G A R
Y C T H C H N Z S W X L M S Z
```

AZARIAH (2 Chronicles 26:20)
CAIN (Genesis 4:16)
DANIEL (Daniel 2:20)
ESTHER (book of Esther)
HAGAR (Genesis 21:17)
ISAIAH (2 Kings 19:5)
JACOB (Genesis 28:5)

JEREMIAH (book of Jeremiah)
JOHN (book of John)
JOSEPH (Genesis 37:28)
MANASSEH (Genesis 46:20)
MORDECAI (Esther 7:10)
NOAH (Genesis 8:1)

PAUL (Acts 16:16)
PETER (John 18:27)
SILAS (Acts 15:22)
STEPHEN (Acts 6:5)
ZEDEKIAH (2 Kings 24:20)

Prisoners and Exiles Part 2

Once again, give yourself 10 points if you find the following names.

```
Z U K X S Q K X S A C U M N C
E L C Z N B A H T X F X I P V
D A N I E L A S E T K A O V S
E L B J A I V I P S C T R X J
K E X X R S H L H H T J P X Q
I U U A A A J A E W B H P T L
A P Z I I E P S N O J O E U N
H A H A G A R R C J B F A R M
G C S A K R H A Q O G P T P O
O I H W S P J P D H L F S A R
T U X H E Y K O E N S W I V D
V Z A S H F G V Y T D P S C E
V O O G E Q G Y U X E M T G C
N J W M A N A S S E H R M K A
V H X C J E R E M I A H G A I
```

AZARIAH	JACOB	NOAH
CAIN	JEREMIAH	PAUL
DANIEL	JOHN	PETER
ESTHER	JOSEPH	SILAS
HAGAR	MANASSEH	STEPHEN
ISAIAH	MORDECAI	ZEDEKIAH

Prisoners and Exiles Part 3

If you find all eighteen names, give yourself 25 points.

```
D J I I S A I A H T N H J B U
O U W K X T E C A P N A R R B
Z C N C R S E H W Z P G Q G I
N O A H A B A P G W Q A M I X
Z O B L R I K H H J T R U T R
Q E I M R Q A D J E E C Q L R
J S D A A I L G P E N P P E D
N A Z E M N J S F P R C T T A
W A C E K A A D Y L Y E H R N
E D R O X I F S C Y P G A W I
Q E P F B K A B S F E D G S E
J F B V X M L H V E J O H N L
O A J M I X U R X E H N E B D
C A I N P I M O R D E C A I W
J O S E P H E S T H E R I M F
```

42

Did You Know?

(SET 5)

A Bible brilliant–worthy set of facts follows.

- There was a man named Dodo in the Bible (Judges 10:1).
- According to the book of Revelation, God's new earth will not have any seas (Revelation 21:1).
- King Ahab built a house made entirely of ivory (1 Kings 22:39).
- The Gadites, the tribe of Gad, had faces like lions (1 Chronicles 12:8).
- King Solomon had black, bushy hair (Song of Solomon 5:11).
- The Sea of Galilee was also known as the Sea of Tiberias (John 21:1).

Who Is?

Identify the following people in this brief but vital test. Correct answers are worth 10 points each.

1. Who is "perfect and upright, and one that feared God"?

2. Who is "the bright and morning star"?

3. Who is "the voice of one crying in the wilderness"?

4. Who is "a rod out of the stem of Jesse"?

5. Who is "my own son in the faith," according to Paul?

6. Who is the "son of the morning"?

7. Who is "the last Adam"?

8. Who is "the salt of the earth," according to Jesus?

9. Who is "a mighty hunter before the Lord"?

10. Who is the "generation of vipers," according to Jesus?

SECTION 3

THE BIBLE BRILLIANT SECTION

This final large section is the Bible scholar section. It has the most difficult challenges but offers the greatest rewards. Expect nothing easy here, but your sense of satisfaction at answering these questions will be the highest of any point during your Bible brilliant experience. (Answers to section 3 begin on page 230.)

> I wish to see the Bible study as much a matter of course in the secular colleges as in the seminary. No educated man can afford to be ignorant of the Bible, and no uneducated man can afford to be ignorant of the Bible.
>
> Theodore Roosevelt, twenty-sixth president
> of the United States

There is nothing in this world that can compare with the Christian fellowship; nothing that can satisfy but Christ.

John D. Rockefeller, American business
magnate and philanthropist

The New Testament is the greatest Book the world has ever known or ever will know.

Charles Dickens, renowned author

Crossword Puzzle

Give yourself 25 bonus points if you solve this crossword puzzle with three or fewer mistakes.

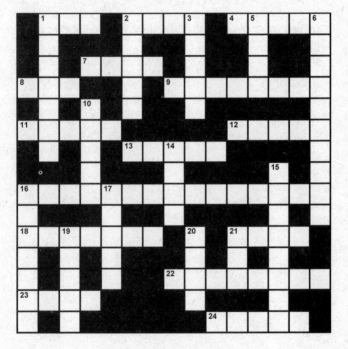

Across

1. "___ is greatly to be feared . . ." (Psalm 89:7)
2. "I have coveted no man's silver, or___" (Acts 20:33)
4. Son of Isaac
7. Eve's husband
8. "Of fowls also of the ___ by sevens" (Genesis 7:3)
9. From 13-Down
11. Savior of the world
12. The "tree" 11-Across hung on
13. "Kingly" version of the Bible
16. The act of having a meal together
18. It should follow a sin
21. ". . . deliver us from ___" (Matthew 6:13)
22. What God has given to all humans
23. It guided the wise men
24. Peter, for one

Down

1. Christ lived there
2. ". . . the ___ of God was upon him" (Luke 2:40)
3. King who was "the sweet psalmist of Israel"
5. "And he said, I heard thy voice in the garden, ___ was afraid, because I was naked; and I hid myself" (Genesis 3:10)
6. Good thing to do with a church group
10. Herod's kingdom
14. Bethlehem visitors
15. Faith
16. Immersion in water
17. 1 or 2 of the Old Testament
19. "And it came to pass in the month ____" (Nehemiah 2:1)
20. Second book of the New Testament
21. Mother of Cain

FOUR GROUPS OF TRIVIA

Each of the following groups of trivia contains fifty questions. Do one group at a time and give yourself 5 points for each correct answer. You may do any or all of the groups as many times as necessary to achieve your goal. Record your score for each group on the score card.

45

Group 1

1. What creature did the ten spies compare themselves to when comparing themselves to the inhabitants of the land of Canaan?
2. Who was the father of Abraham?
3. What animal skins that were dyed red were used as offerings to help make the tabernacle?
4. After Pilate could find no guilt in Jesus, why did the Jews say that Jesus should die?
5. How were Joseph and Mary warned that someone wanted to kill the baby Jesus?
6. To whom was Paul writing when he wrote, "I will receive you. And will be a Father unto you, and ye shall be my sons and daughters, saith the Lord Almighty"?
7. How did the sailors learn that Jonah was responsible for the storm?
8. In a parable told by Jesus, what two men went up to the temple to pray?
9. What part of King Asa's body was diseased?
10. What servant had his ear cut off during Jesus's arrest?
11. In what Jewish month is the Passover?
12. Paul and Silas were imprisoned in what city during their second missionary journey?

13. What did Samson carry to the top of the hill overlooking Hebron?

14. What priest anointed Solomon?

15. Whom did Daniel see sitting on a throne in his vision of the four beasts?

16. How many sons did Gideon have?

17. What is the shortest book in the Old Testament?

18. Whose house did Paul enter in Caesarea?

19. The Ethiopian eunuch held what office under Candace, the queen of the Ethiopians?

20. According to Matthew, what was the first of the Beatitudes of the Sermon on the Mount?

21. On what day of creation did God create trees and vegetation?

22. What disciple asked Jesus to show him the Father?

23. Who dozed off during one of Paul's sermons and fell out of a window?

24. Psalm 100 states that we should come before the Lord's presence with what?

25. After his resurrection, Jesus appeared to his disciples at what sea?

26. Paul preached during his first missionary journey on what island?

27. When Athaliah saw her son Ahaziah was dead, what did she do?

28. What prophet told Naaman to wash in the Jordan River to cure his leprosy?

29. How many concubines did Solomon have?

30. How many wise men does the Bible say came to visit Jesus?

31. What was Priscilla's occupation?

32. Who had a bed 9 cubits (13.5 feet) long by 4 cubits (6 feet) wide?

33. How did Moses make the acrid waters of Marah drinkable?

34. What does El Shaddai, a name for God, mean?

35. What did Samson offer as a reward to the Philistines if they could solve his riddle?

36. Where did Philip preach about the kingdom of God, leading many to become baptized?

37. Whose handkerchiefs could heal the sick?

38. Were Adam and Eve ashamed about their nakedness at first?

39. How many of Nineveh's inhabitants weren't able to discern between their right hand and their left hand?

40. When Paul got his sight back, what did he do next?

41. What is the seventh commandment?

42. How many cities of refuge were on the east side of Jordan?

43. What did an angel throw into the sea representing the throwing down of Babylon?

44. In what city did Elijah raise a widow's son from the dead?

45. What Old Testament prophet was given a book to eat by God?

46. As God calls us to a life of holiness, what are we doing if we ignore this advice?

47. Who was the centurion who watched over Paul on his journey to Rome?

48. Who said, "To obey is better than sacrifice"?

49. What sort of man was Noah, according to the Bible?

50. How did Paul escape from Damascus?

Group 2

1. Who was given the Spirit of God, enabling him to become a competent craftsman and help with the building of the tabernacle?
2. Bread of deceit is sweet to a man, but what will his mouth be filled with afterward?
3. What is bound in the heart of a child?
4. How old was Abraham's first wife, Sarah, when she died?
5. What prophet told Jeroboam he would rule over ten tribes?
6. What did Melchizedek supply to Abram?
7. In a vision, what did Zechariah see destroying the houses of thieves and liars?
8. How was Lois related to Timothy?
9. The prophecy involving seventy weeks refers to what awaited event?
10. How many years did it take for Solomon to build his own house?
11. What were the disciples arguing about when Jesus told them he would judge the twelve tribes in the kingdom?
12. What occurred when the third vial of wrath was poured on the earth?
13. Anna the prophetess belonged to what tribe?
14. At what battle were the Israelites defeated because Joshua did not first seek the Lord's guidance?

15. As part of the high priest's garments, on what type of stone were the twelve tribes of Israel to have their names engraved?

16. In what city was Lydia converted?

17. Jephthah led Israel against what enemy army?

18. In the parable of the debtors, while one owed five hundred denarii, the other owed how much?

19. The fifth trumpet plague in the book of Revelation is like what plague that was also delivered on Egypt?

20. What prophet prophesied that Paul would be bound in Jerusalem?

21. Who was the father-in-law of Caiaphas, the high priest at the time of Jesus's crucifixion?

22. For how long did the son of Hillel, Abdon, judge Israel?

23. What four beasts did Daniel see in a vision?

24. Whom did Paul take along with him on his first missionary journey?

25. When Jesus sent out the disciples to preach for the first time, to whom did he send them?

26. How many palm trees were in Elim when the Israelites arrived?

27. Wisdom is more precious than which valuable gems?

28. How many rivers did the river in Eden split into outside of the garden?

29. What did the Israelites borrow from their neighbors, the Egyptians?

30. Where will the believers reign in the kingdom of God?

31. Who went into labor and had a child after hearing that the ark of God had been captured and her father-in-law and husband were both dead?

32. What sorcerer did Paul meet on the island of Cyprus?

33. Who arrived in Galilee preaching about the kingdom of God?

34. Joseph's brothers sold him to what kind of people?

35. Who does the prayer of faith save?

36. Pharaoh gave the Egyptian name Zaphnathpaaneah to what person?

37. Where did Delilah live?

38. Who thanked King David for allowing David's son Absalom to return to Jerusalem?

39. Who was Paul speaking about when he said, "The Lord give mercy unto the house of Onesiphorus; for he oft refreshed me, and was not ashamed of my chain"?

40. According to Jesus, what would the twelve apostles receive for forsaking everything and following him?

41. According to the book of Job, what is the hope of a tree that is cut down?

42. Initially, how was the earth watered before rain?

43. What group of many said, "Worthy is the Lamb that was slain"?

44. What feast came into existence when Queen Esther saved the Jews from destruction?

45. What fraction of his goods did Zacchaeus give away to the poor?

46. In answering his prayers, who gave water to the camels of Abraham's servant?

47. How old was Anna the prophetess when she first saw Jesus?

48. What book states that Jesus is the bread of life?

49. What offering did Gideon present to the Lord under an oak tree?

50. Abraham buried his wife in what field?

Group 3

1. What did Rachel steal from her father when she left home with Jacob?
2. An excellent wife is what to her husband?
3. What psalm mentions a snail?
4. Samson belonged to what tribe?
5. Why did Pharaoh give Joseph's family land in Goshen?
6. Who was the first man to pass by the wounded man in the parable of the good Samaritan?
7. Balaam and his donkey are in what book of the Bible?
8. Why should children listen to the instruction of a father?
9. What did Jesus eat to convince the disciples that he really had been raised from the dead?
10. How old was Joseph when he died?
11. Jesus said not to swear by your head because you cannot do what?
12. What is acceptable to God because of the Word of God and prayer?
13. According to Proverbs, how shall a man's belly be satisfied?
14. What did God make on the fourth day?
15. Where was King David born?
16. In the good father parable, if a son asks for an egg, what does the good father not give him?
17. How were the Thessalonians told to keep their own bodies?

18. How many companions did the Philistines give to Samson at the feast in Timnah?

19. Psalm 90:1 is a prayer of what famous person?

20. How long did Noah live after the flood?

21. What musical instruments were played to praise God when the temple foundation was rebuilt?

22. How many years did Jacob live?

23. What brother did Joseph send to prison while his other brothers returned home to Jacob?

24. Whom did the Lord command to walk barefoot and naked for three years?

25. How many silver shekels did Jeremiah pay to Hanameel to purchase a field in Anathoth?

26. In the Song of Solomon, the woman's hair is described as a flock of what animal?

27. What was the first offering made to the Lord in the book of Genesis?

28. In the fig tree parable, what was near when one saw a tree putting forth leaves?

29. Who has the right to the tree of life, according to the book of Revelation?

30. The book of Proverbs says that those seeking death acquire their wealth by doing what?

31. What was the color of the high priest's robe?

32. What does the name Israel mean?

33. When building a new house, what was an Israelite to do?

34. What prophet said, "I loved him, and called my son out of Egypt"?

35. What killed twenty-seven thousand Syrians in the city of Aphek?

36. What was the weight of the gold that Solomon acquired in a single year?
37. Who was killed by a thick cloth dipped in water?
38. According to Ezekiel's prophecy, who was the mother of Jerusalem?
39. According to James, what should we do after confessing our faults to one another?
40. The disciple Tabitha was also known by what name?
41. What book of the Bible contains the story of David and Goliath?
42. It is better to obtain wisdom than what?
43. What did the Holy Spirit appear as when the disciples received him?
44. What water creatures were deemed unclean?
45. Which of Leah's sons brought her mandrakes?
46. Why was David forbidden to build God's house?
47. Zipporah was married to what man?
48. Who dreamed of a tree that grew all the way to heaven?
49. Who was King Jehu's father?
50. The inscription "Jesus of Nazareth, King of the Jews" on the cross of Jesus was written in what three languages?

Group 4

1. Who had his sight restored by Ananias in Damascus?
2. In Numbers, what two men had an army of 603,554 for war in Israel?
3. Who leapt inside his mother's womb when Mary paid a visit?
4. When David was anointed the king of Israel, how old was he?
5. Who said, "But as for me and my house, we will serve the LORD"?
6. To receive the crown of life, what does one need to do, according to the book of Revelation?
7. Both the longest and the shortest chapter in the Bible can be found in what book?
8. How old was Abraham when his son Isaac was born?
9. How many rivers were formed from the river that flowed out of Eden?
10. How tall was Goliath?
11. When Jesus said, "Get thee behind me, Satan," to whom was he talking?
12. The disciples were called Christians for the first time in what city?
13. According to Paul, what is the fulfillment of the law?
14. Who helped the battered Jesus carry his cross?

15. Moses belonged to what tribe of Israel?

16. In Revelation, what was the name of the city of God?

17. To what king did Isaac claim that Rebekah was his sister, not his wife?

18. After he killed an Egyptian, to what land did Moses flee?

19. Who was Abraham's second wife?

20. What three women, along with other unnamed women, discovered the empty tomb of Jesus?

21. Of the two brothers, Moses and Aaron, which one was older?

22. What two books of the Bible are named after women?

23. The first two disciples chosen by Jesus were what two brothers?

24. Who ate honey out of the carcass of a lion?

25. Of the twelve tribes of Israel, which was forbidden to own land in Canaan?

26. What historical relics did Moses take from Egypt during the time of the exodus?

27. What was the sign of the covenant between Abraham and God?

28. Who, according to the book of Judges, was a good old age when he died?

29. What was the city of David?

30. Who was Manasseh's and Ephraim's father?

31. Who adopted the baby Moses?

32. Who was chosen to be Moses's spokesperson?

33. What two creatures in the Bible spoke to humans?

34. Moses was taking care of the flock of what man when he came across the burning bush?

35. After Jesus's miracle in which he fed five thousand with five loaves of bread and two fish, how much food was left over?

36. Who was described by God as a blameless and upright man?

37. How many demons were cast out of Mary Magdalene?

38. How old was Abraham when he was circumcised?

39. Who replaced Judas as the twelfth apostle?

40. When Cain was forced to leave Eden, where did he go?

41. When Jesus said, "Man shall not live by bread alone," to whom was he speaking?

42. How long had Lazarus been dead before being raised by Jesus?

43. How many hours did Jesus suffer on the cross before saying, "My God, my God, why hast thou forsaken me?"

44. According to the book of John, it was not Jesus but whom who baptized?

45. Where was Moses buried?

46. Who was the third son of Adam and Eve?

47. The twelve gates of the new Jerusalem were made from what gems?

48. Cain was the founder of what city?

49. How many righteous people exist, according to Paul?

50. How long did Adam live?

Fulfilled Prophecies about Jesus

In the following exercise, an Old Testament prophecy about Jesus is listed. You must name the New Testament book(s) in which the prophecy was fulfilled. In some cases, more than one New Testament book mentions the same prophecy. Give yourself 20 points for each prophecy for which you correctly identify the New Testament book or books.

You do not need to provide the verse to get a correct answer in this section, only the book(s), although it is an excellent idea to try to memorize as many verses as you can.

You may do this section as many times as you wish and record only your highest score on the score card.

1. The Messiah would be born of a virgin. Old Testament: Isaiah 7:14, New Testament (2 books): _____ and _____

2. A messenger would prepare the way for the Messiah. Old Testament: Isaiah 40:3–5, New Testament: _____

3. The Messiah would be born of a woman. Old Testament: Genesis 3:15, New Testament (2 books): _____ and _____

4. Jesus would be declared the Son of God. Old Testament: Psalm 2:7, New Testament: _____

5. The Messiah would be born in Bethlehem. Old Testament: Micah 5:2, New Testament (2 books): _____ and _____

6. Jesus would be called King. Old Testament: Psalm 2:6, New Testament (2 books): _____ and _____

7. Jesus's throne will be eternal. Old Testament: Psalm 45:6–7 and Daniel 2:44, New Testament (2 books): _____ and _____

8. The Messiah would come from the tribe of Judah. Old Testament: Genesis 49:10, New Testament (2 books): _____ and _____

9. The Savior would come from the line of Abraham. Old Testament: Genesis 12:3 and Genesis 22:18, New Testament (2 books): _____ and _____

10. The Messiah would come to heal the brokenhearted. Old Testament: Isaiah 61:1–2, New Testament: _____

11. The Messiah would spend a season in Egypt. Old Testament: Hosea 11:1, New Testament: _____

12. The Savior would be crucified with criminals. Old Testament: Isaiah 53:12, New Testament: _____

13. The Messiah would be heir to King David's throne. Old Testament: 2 Samuel 7:12–13 and Isaiah 9:7, New Testament (2 books): _____ and _____

14. Jesus would be rejected by his own people. Old Testament: Psalm 69:8 and Isaiah 53:3, New Testament (1 book, 2 chapters): _____ and _____

15. The Messiah would be called Emmanuel. Old Testament: Isaiah 7:14, New Testament: _____

16. The Savior would be given vinegar to drink. Old Testament: Psalm 69:21, New Testament (2 books): _____ and _____

17. The Messiah would be a prophet. Old Testament: Deuteronomy 18:15, New Testament: _____

18. The Messiah would be called a Nazarene. Old Testament: Isaiah 11:1, New Testament: _____

19. The Messiah would be praised by little children. Old Testament: Psalm 8:2, New Testament: _____

20. Jesus would be spat upon and struck. Old Testament: Isaiah 50:6, New Testament: _____

21. The Savior would be hated without cause. Old Testament: Psalm 35:19 and Psalm 69:4, New Testament: _____

22. The Messiah would be mocked, teased, and ridiculed. Old Testament: Psalm 22:7–8, New Testament: _____

23. The Messiah would come from the line of Isaac. Old Testament: Genesis 17:19 and Genesis 21:12, New Testament: _____

24. Jesus would be a sacrifice for sin. Old Testament: Isaiah 53:5–12, New Testament: _____

25. The Messiah would speak in parables. Old Testament: Psalm 78:2–4 and Isaiah 6:9–10, New Testament:

_____

26. The Savior would be betrayed. Old Testament: Psalm 41:9 and Zechariah 11:12–13, New Testament (2 books): _____ and _____

27. Jesus's bones would not be broken during his crucifixion. Exodus 12:46 and Psalm 34:20, New Testament:

    _____

28. Jesus's hands and feet would be pierced. Old Testament: Psalm 22:16 and Zechariah 12:10, New Testament:

    _____

29. The Messiah would be falsely accused. Old Testament: Psalm 35:11, New Testament: _____

30. Jesus would be silent before his accusers. Old Testament: Isaiah 53:7, New Testament: _____

31. Soldiers would gamble for the Messiah's garments. Old Testament: Psalm 22:18, New Testament (2 books): _____ and _____

32. The Messiah would be forsaken by God. Old Testament: Psalm 22:1, New Testament: _____

33. Soldiers would pierce Jesus in his side. Old Testament: Zechariah 12:10, New Testament: _____

34. The Messiah would be resurrected from the dead. Old Testament: Psalm 16:10 and Psalm 49:15, New Testament (2 books): _____ and _____

35. The Savior would ascend to heaven. Old Testament: Psalm 24:7–10, New Testament (2 books): _____ and _____

36. The Messiah would be seated at the right hand of the Father. Old Testament: Psalm 68:18 and Psalm 110:1, New Testament (2 books): _____ and _____

50

The Fast 100

Here are one hundred trivia questions called the "fast" 100 because the answers should pop into your mind relatively quickly. Give yourself 1 point for each correct answer.

1. What garden did Jesus go to before being falsely arrested?
2. While a storm raged, what was Jonah doing on board a ship at the time?
3. When Joseph was in Egypt, who was his master?
4. When Herod was killing babies in Bethlehem, where did Mary and Joseph go?
5. When the priests blew their trumpets, what happened to the city of Jericho?
6. What land was promised to Abram by the Lord?
7. What event aided in the release of Paul and Silas from prison?
8. How many plagues did God inflict on Egypt?
9. What did King Solomon request when God appeared to him in a dream?
10. In the Old Testament, how were sins forgiven?
11. In what form did the Lord appear to Moses?
12. According to the Bible, what should we seek first?
13. Which of Jacob's wives does the Bible say he loved the most?

14. In what manner were the Thessalonians told to pray?

15. What were the commandments given to Moses kept in?

16. According to the Bible, what is the best place to pray?

17. What did God breathe into Adam's nostrils?

18. Who wrote the book of Revelation?

19. How long was Jonah stuck inside a great fish?

20. Who was Hagar's son?

21. When Moses was receiving the Ten Commandments from God, what were the Israelites doing?

22. Whom did God tell to leave his home and family and travel to an unknown country?

23. What two things guided the Israelites in the wilderness?

24. How old was Jesus when he began his ministry?

25. The sinful man Balaam was spoken to by what creature?

26. Who was the first woman Jacob married?

27. Who, through the power of God, parted the Red Sea?

28. When Pilate asked the unruly crowd what prisoner should be released, whom did they choose?

29. Who married Abram?

30. Who baptized Jesus?

31. What angel appeared to Mary?

32. When Abraham's servant went looking for a wife for Isaac, whom did he find?

33. To whom was Jesus talking when he said, "Why are ye fearful, O ye of little faith?"

34. Where did the man who received one talent hide it?

35. Jacob agreed to work seven years of hard labor to win the hand in marriage of what woman?

36. What woman promised the Lord that if she were blessed with a son she would dedicate the boy to him?

37. When Jesus was born, in what was he wrapped?

38. What was the name of David's first wife?

39. When Jesus asked the disciples, "But whom say ye that I am?" what was Peter's reply?

40. In the parable of the ten virgins, for what were the virgins waiting?

41. Who could be considered the stepfather of Jesus?

42. After the death of Naomi's husband and sons, who stayed with her?

43. Who lied and claimed that Joseph had tried to commit adultery with her?

44. How did God curse the serpent that deceived Eve?

45. What was the name of Moses's wife?

46. Who betrayed Jesus with a kiss?

47. In the book of Genesis, in what way did God say mankind was similar to him?

48. When Jesus gave his Sermon on the Mount, what did he say about tomorrow?

49. Whose name did God change to Israel?

50. How should we treat the rich and the poor, according to James?

51. Where was Jesus baptized?

52. After Jesus was crucified, who led the church?

53. According to James, what happens when we draw nigh (near) to God?

54. Who was taken captive into Egypt but later saved the entire country from famine?

55. What holiday is referred to as resurrection day?

56. When an adulteress was accused by a crowd, what was Jesus's response?

57. What woman betrayed Samson to the Philistines by persuading him to reveal the secret of his incredible strength?

58. Who spoke the words, "My soul doth magnify the Lord"?

59. Who tried to tempt Jesus by saying, "If thou be the Son of God, command that these stones be made bread"?

60. Who was converted to Christianity on the road to Damascus?

61. What does Eve's name mean?

62. What Israelite became the queen of Persia?

63. What evil queen wanted to kill the prophet Elijah?

64. How did the height-challenged Zacchaeus manage to see Jesus in a crowd?

65. Who sold his birthright to his brother for a hot meal?

66. Who gave birth to Moses?

67. Who could interpret King Nebuchadnezzar's dream?

68. Who was turned into a pillar of salt after being warned not to look back at Sodom and Gomorrah?

69. Who was the sister-in-law of Ruth?

70. Why did Adam hide himself from the Lord?

71. After refusing to eat the food of the king, who gained the ability to interpret visions and dreams?

72. What does Emmanuel mean?

73. What kind of wood did Noah use to build the ark?

74. Who advised Joseph that Jesus would be the Savior who would save his people from their sins?

75. Why was David so confident that he could defeat Goliath?

76. In what sermon did Jesus deliver the Beatitudes?

77. After Aaron put his staff into the tabernacle, what was produced on it?

78. What form did the Holy Spirit take during Jesus's baptism?

79. Who said, "This is my beloved Son, in whom I am well pleased"?

80. What happened to those whose names were not written in the book of life?

81. Where did Jesus miraculously walk on water?

82. Before he exiled them from the Garden of Eden, what did God do to Adam and Eve?

83. The prophet Hosea was commanded to marry what harlot?

84. What was the name of Sarah's handmaiden?

85. How did Jonah feel about the way the people of Nineveh responded to his message about God?

86. After Moses died, who became the leader of the children of Israel?

87. According to Jesus, how should we receive the kingdom of God?

88. What happened to Daniel after he gave thanks to the Lord by an open window?

89. Who was jealous of the prodigal son?

90. Who could be heard from heaven after the baptism of Jesus Christ?

91. What position did Zacchaeus hold?

92. When Joseph was in prison, for what trait did he become known?

93. Why did Jesus choose to use parables in his teaching?

94. In the book of Genesis, people traveled from many countries to Egypt to buy what food item?

95. Who told Jesus, "All these things will I give thee, if thou wilt fall down and worship me"?

96. How did a man inflicted with palsy at Capernaum gain access to the house in which Jesus preached?

97. Who refused to believe that Jesus was resurrected until he saw him with his own eyes?

98. Which one of Joseph's brothers did Jacob not allow to travel to Egypt?

99. What did God place in the Garden of Eden to protect the tree of life?

100. According to the Bible, what is "the least of all the seeds: but when it is grown, it is the greatest among herbs"?

TRIVIA BY TOPIC

In the following section, complete each multiple-choice quiz and give yourself 2 points for each correct answer.

51

Who Asked?

1. Who asked, "Am I my brother's keeper?"
   A. Joseph
   B. Jacob
   C. Cain
   D. Esau

2. Who wanted to know, "What wilt thou give me, seeing I go childless?"
   A. Sarah
   B. Abram
   C. Leah
   D. Jacob

3. Who inquired, "Shall not the Judge of all the earth do right?"
   A. Joshua
   B. Nahum
   C. Abraham
   D. Micah

4. Who asked, "Why is it that thou hast sent me?"
   A. Moses
   B. Joshua
   C. Matthew
   D. Joseph

5. Who asked the Lord, "LORD God, whereby shall I know that I shall inherit it?"
   A. Thomas
   B. Jacob
   C. Peter
   D. Abram

6. Who inquired, "Why is my pain perpetual, and my wound incurable?"
   A. Jeremiah
   B. Isaiah
   C. Jehoshaphat
   D. Isaac

7. Who said, "Why dost thou shew me iniquity, and cause me to behold grievance?"
   A. Solomon
   B. Habakkuk
   C. Amos
   D. Pharaoh

8. What men asked, "Shall one man sin, and wilt thou be wroth with all the congregation?"
   A. Moses and Aaron
   B. Cain and Abel
   C. Paul and Timothy
   D. Peter and John

9. Who wanted to know, "Ah, LORD God! wilt thou make a full end of the remnant of Israel?"
   A. Jeremiah
   B. Hezekiah
   C. Ezekiel
   D. Zephaniah

10. Who asked, "Behold, when I come unto the children of Israel, and shall say unto them, The God of your fathers hath sent me unto you; and they shall say to me, What is his name? what shall I say unto them?"
    A. Aaron
    B. Jacob
    C. Moses
    D. Abraham

11. Who inquired, "Behold, I am vile; what shall I answer thee?"
    A. Paul
    B. Job
    C. Nathan
    D. Simon

12. Who asked, "Shall I go and smite these Philistines?"
    A. Moses
    B. Elijah
    C. Samson
    D. David

52

Hearing from God

1. Who was called to build a ship?
   A. Jonah
   B. Esau
   C. Noah
   D. Abram

2. Who was called to leave his home for a strange land?
   A. Jonah
   B. Esau
   C. Noah
   D. Abram

3. Who was Israel's first high priest?
   A. Joshua
   B. Moses
   C. Caleb
   D. Aaron

4. What man was called by God to be king over the ten tribes of Israel?
   A. Solomon
   B. David
   C. Saul
   D. Jeroboam

5. What prophet raised a widow's son from the dead?
   A. Jonah
   B. Daniel
   C. Elijah
   D. Elisha

6. Who freed the Israelites from Egyptian bondage?
   A. Joshua
   B. Moses
   C. Caleb
   D. Aaron

7. Who was called to
   receive God's covenant
   of peace for his family?

   A. Eleazar
   B. Phinehas
   C. Joshua
   D. Moses

8. Who dreamed he would
   have authority over his
   brothers?

   A. Esau
   B. Jacob
   C. Joseph
   D. Isaac

53

Bible Brilliant Level

1. What is the shortest verse in the Bible?
   A. 1 John 1:35
   B. Luke 11:35
   C. John 11:35
   D. 1 Chronicles 1:1

2. Who washed his steps with butter?
   A. John
   B. Job
   C. Jonah
   D. Joshua

3. What person with the occupation of dressmaker was raised from the dead?
   A. Dinah
   B. Diane
   C. Dorcas
   D. Deborah

4. How many households did Joshua leave undisturbed in Jericho?
   A. 1
   B. 2
   C. 3
   D. 4

5. Who in Genesis wept when he kissed his sweetheart?
   A. Jacob
   B. Esau
   C. Laban
   D. Abraham

6. What man infamously killed sixty-nine of his brothers?
   A. Gideon
   B. Abimelech
   C. Joshua
   D. Absalom

7. What was the common thing shared by Samson, David, and Benaiah the son of Jehoiada?
   A. They all had eight wives
   B. They all killed a lion
   C. They were all rugged and handsome
   D. None of the above

8. Who killed six hundred men with an ox goad?
   A. Sisera
   B. Shamgar
   C. Shimshai
   D. Shishak

9. Who possessed hair like eagle feathers and fingernails similar to bird claws?
   A. Nebushazban
   B. Onesiphorus
   C. Melchishua
   D. Nebuchadnezzar

10. From what material was the covering for the tent over the tabernacle made?
    A. Ram skins
    B. Shittim wood
    C. Wheat and barley sacks
    D. Fig leaves

11. What did Elisha do when he learned that Jericho had bad water?
    A. He prayed
    B. He fasted and prayed
    C. He threw salt into it
    D. He poured a bowl of sugar in it

12. What two books of the Bible were written for Theophilus?
    A. Matthew and Mark
    B. Mark and Luke
    C. Luke and John
    D. Luke and Acts

13. What was the name of King Saul's wife?
    A. Salome
    B. Anna
    C. Ahinoam
    D. Sarah

14. Who stopped the Israelites from burning incense to the bronze snake that Moses made?
    A. Samuel
    B. Hezekiah
    C. Aaron
    D. Jeremiah

15. What book of the Bible mentions a synagogue of Satan?
    A. Daniel
    B. John
    C. Revelation
    D. Joel

16. What biblical character claimed that laughter is mad?
    A. David
    B. Saul
    C. Solomon
    D. Jonathan

17. How many years were the Israelites in Egypt?
    A. 40
    B. 365
    C. 400
    D. 430

18. How many angels will be stationed at the gates of the new Jerusalem?
    A. 10
    B. 12
    C. 15
    D. 20

19. How many years did God add to Hezekiah's life?
    A. 10
    B. 12
    C. 15
    D. 20

20. How many men mentioned in the Bible had the name Judas?
    A. 1
    B. 3
    C. 6
    D. 11

Anything Goes

1. How many people were saved in Noah's ark?
   A. 5
   B. 6
   C. 7
   D. 8

2. What was the name of the first woman judge in Israel?
   A. Dorcas
   B. Salome
   C. Priscilla
   D. Deborah

3. What was the name of the angel who revealed to Mary that she would be the mother of Jesus?
   A. Michael
   B. Gabriel
   C. John
   D. Joelah

4. How many stories or levels were in Noah's ark?
   A. 2
   B. 3
   C. 4
   D. 5

5. Who escaped from Damascus in a basket?
   A. Paul
   B. Peter
   C. John
   D. Thomas

6. Who interpreted Pharaoh's dream as seven good years and seven lean years in Egypt?
   A. Joseph
   B. Paul
   C. Daniel
   D. John

7. Who was killed when they lied to the Holy Spirit?

   A. Aquila and Priscilla

   B. Boaz and Ruth

   C. Ananias and Sapphira

   D. Abraham and Sarah

8. What was the name of the queen who was devoured by dogs?

   A. Esther

   B. Vashti

   C. Jezebel

   D. Sheba

9. What does the word *Ichabod* mean?

   A. The glory is departed

   B. The glory is revealed

   C. The glory is prepared

   D. The glory is recognized

10. Who asked God to put his tears in a bottle?

    A. Saul

    B. Jonathan

    C. David

    D. Samuel

11. What was the name of Ruth's father-in-law?

    A. Elhanan

    B. Eliakim

    C. Eliezer

    D. Elimelech

12. What king in the Bible had the longest reign?

    A. Saul

    B. David

    C. Manasseh

    D. Josiah

13. What queen came from a far land to experience the wisdom of King Solomon?

    A. Queen Esther

    B. Queen Vashti

    C. The queen of Sheba

    D. Queen Jezebel

14. Who wore clothes made out of camel's hair?

    A. John the Baptist

    B. Paul

    C. Peter

    D. Jesus

15. Paul was blind for how many days while in Damascus?
    A. 0
    B. 3
    C. 12
    D. 40

16. Who said, "Divide the living child in two, give half to one, and half to the other"?
    A. King David
    B. King Josiah
    C. King Solomon
    D. King Saul

17. Who came to Jesus by night to talk with him?
    A. Simon
    B. Lazarus
    C. Nicodemus
    D. John

18. Who was released from prison by an angel?
    A. Peter
    B. John
    C. Paul
    D. Silas

19. According to 1 Peter 3:20, referring to the ark, how many souls were saved by water?
    A. None
    B. 8
    C. Every soul forever
    D. 144,000

20. What woman was the wife of both Nabal and King David?
    A. Bathsheba
    B. Michal
    C. Rebekah
    D. Abigail

21. Who was Nebuchadnezzar's son?
    A. Belshazzar
    B. Sheshbazzar
    C. Meshezabel
    D. Hammolecheth

22. What runaway slave eventually returned to his master?
    A. Belshazzar
    B. Onesimus
    C. Meshezabel
    D. Hammolecheth

23. What king stayed in his bed and pouted because he could not purchase another person's vineyard?
    A. King David
    B. King Saul
    C. King Ahab
    D. King Solomon

24. In a dream, what did Abimelech learn about Sarah?
    A. She was married
    B. She was single
    C. She was divorced
    D. She was a widow

25. How many times did Noah send a dove out of the ark to try to find land?
    A. 1
    B. 2
    C. 3
    D. 4

26. Whose ten sons were hung on the same gallows as he?
    A. Achin's
    B. Haman's
    C. Absalom's
    D. Bigthan's

27. What member of Pharaoh's staff was hung for theft?
    A. The cook
    B. The chief baker
    C. The cupbearer
    D. The musician

28. What king did Bigthan and Teresh plan to assassinate?
    A. King Ahasuerus
    B. King Elah
    C. King Saul
    D. King David

29. What was not in Solomon's house because Solomon considered it to be of little value?
    A. Brass
    B. Garnet
    C. Silver
    D. Pearls

30. What did Solomon do when he got older?
    A. Divorced his seven hundred wives
    B. Became closer to the Lord
    C. Started worshiping false gods
    D. Enjoyed fasting and praying more

31. How many times was Paul stoned?
    A. Once
    B. Twice
    C. Three times
    D. None

32. What group of people believed in the resurrection and in angels?
    A. Sadducees
    B. Pharisees
    C. Jews
    D. Romans

33. Who was Solomon's son?
    A. Rehoboam
    B. Rehob
    C. Regem-Melech
    D. Rehabiah

34. How many sons and daughters did Solomon's son have?
    A. 21 sons and 50 daughters
    B. 28 sons and 60 daughters
    C. 22 sons and 40 daughters
    D. 25 sons and 75 daughters

35. From what material was the covering for the tent over the tabernacle made?
    A. Ram skins
    B. Shittim wood
    C. Wheat and barley sacks
    D. Fig leaves

36. What did Elisha do when he learned of the bad water in Jericho?
    A. He prayed
    B. He left the city
    C. He threw salt into it
    D. He made a mud mixture

37. People weren't given permission to do what until after the flood?
    A. Take baths
    B. Eat meat
    C. Make fires
    D. Comb their hair

38. What two books of the Bible were written for Theophilus?
    A. Matthew and Mark
    B. Mark and Luke
    C. Luke and John
    D. Luke and Acts

39. What was the name of King Saul's wife?
    A. Salome
    B. Anna
    C. Ahinoam
    D. Sarah

40. Who stopped the Israelites from burning incense to the bronze snake that Moses made?
    A. Samuel
    B. Hezekiah
    C. Aaron
    D. Jeremiah

41. What book of the Bible mentions a synagogue of Satan?
    A. Daniel
    B. John
    C. Revelation
    D. Joel

42. What person in the Bible claimed that laughter is mad?
    A. David
    B. Saul
    C. Solomon
    D. Jonathan

43. How many years were the Israelites in Egypt?
    A. 40
    B. 365
    C. 400
    D. 430

44. How many angels will stand at the gates of the new Jerusalem?
    A. 10
    B. 12
    C. 15
    D. 20

45. How many years did
    God add to Hezekiah's
    life?
    A. 10
    B. 12
    C. 15
    D. 20

46. How many men in the
    Bible had the name
    Judas?
    A. 4
    B. 5
    C. 6
    D. 7

Royalty

1. How many wives did Solomon have?
   A. 500
   B. 600
   C. 700
   D. 800

2. What future king of Israel was anointed by Samuel?
   A. Saul
   B. Solomon
   C. Uzziah
   D. Joash

3. To please his foreign wives, who built pagan temples?
   A. Saul
   B. Darius
   C. David
   D. Solomon

4. Of what was Paul a maker?
   A. Ships
   B. Tents
   C. Idols
   D. Gallows

5. Who infamously created a golden calf?
   A. Gilead
   B. Demetrius
   C. Moses
   D. Aaron

6. When Jesus was arrested, what king demanded that Jesus prove himself by performing miracles?
   A. Hiram
   B. Herod
   C. Agag
   D. Ahab

7. Who was the last king of Judah?
   A. Zedekiah
   B. Hezekiah
   C. Tirhakah
   D. Hazael

8. Who was in charge of all the bronze work in the temple?
   A. Haramn
   B. Hiram
   C. Hunram
   D. Haran

9. What king held a banquet in which a hand left a message on the palace wall?
   A. Jabin
   B. Achish
   C. Herod
   D. Belshazzar

10. What leader of his people created a brass snake?
    A. Joshua
    B. Gideon
    C. Moses
    D. Abimelech

Firsts

1. Whom did Jesus choose to be his first disciple(s)?
   A. Simon Peter and Andrew
   B. Matthew
   C. James
   D. John

2. Who was the first judge of Israel?
   A. Deborah
   B. Othniel
   C. Ruth
   D. Aaron

3. Who was the first man to be exiled alone, without a mate?
   A. Esau
   B. Ishmael
   C. Cain
   D. Joseph

4. Who constructed the first altar?
   A. Noah
   B. Solomon
   C. Abraham
   D. Abel

5. Who wore the first bridal veil?
   A. Michal
   B. Sarah
   C. Rebekah
   D. Rachel

6. Who was the wearer of the first ring mentioned in the Bible?
   A. Abraham
   B. Abimelech
   C. Jacob
   D. Pharaoh

7. Who was the Bible's first crop farmer?

   A. Abel

   B. Cain

   C. Noah

   D. Shem

8. Who was the first priest mentioned in Scripture?

   A. Jethro

   B. Zecharias

   C. Aaron

   D. Melchizedek

9. Who was the Bible's first shepherdess?

   A. Rachel

   B. Abigail

   C. Anna

   D. Eve

10. Who were the first foreign missionaries revealed in Scripture?

    A. Peter and John

    B. Paul and Silas

    C. Aquila and Priscilla

    D. Paul and Barnabas

Random Bible Trivia

1. Who preached at Pentecost?
   A. Paul
   B. Peter
   C. Barnabas
   D. Philip

2. In Revelation, what church was described as neither hot nor cold?
   A. The church of Laodicea
   B. The church of Sardis
   C. The church of Philadelphia
   D. The church of Thyatira

3. By what other name was the disciple Matthew known?
   A. James
   B. Simon
   C. Levi
   D. John

4. Who reluctantly denied he knew Christ?
   A. John
   B. Paul
   C. Peter
   D. James

5. How many times did Moses strike the rock at Kadesh before water gushed forth?
   A. 1
   B. 2
   C. 7
   D. 13

6. Who had a vision of the Ancient of days seated on a throne?
   A. David
   B. Joshua
   C. Daniel
   D. Jonah

7. A multitude of what bird appeared miraculously and became food for the Israelites during the exodus?
   A. Quail
   B. Raven
   C. Eagle
   D. Duck

8. The words of what prophet caused the Syrian soldiers to be struck blind?
   A. Elisha
   B. Jeremiah
   C. Isaiah
   D. Elijah

9. What man said, "For in him we live, and move, and have our being"?
   A. Jacob
   B. Paul
   C. David
   D. Ruth

10. What Bible book includes a passage that advises sleepers to rise from the dead?
    A. 1 Corinthians
    B. Romans
    C. Ephesians
    D. Acts

11. Who hurled a javelin at David?
    A. Absalom
    B. Saul
    C. Uzziah
    D. Abner

12. How many angels were sent to save Lot and his family from the wicked city of Sodom?
    A. 2
    B. 3
    C. 4
    D. 5

13. Where was Jesus when he was strengthened by an angel sent by the Father?
    A. The wilderness
    B. Garden of Gethsemane
    C. Mount Carmel
    D. Lystra

14. What river was turned into blood?
    A. Gihon
    B. Jordan
    C. Nile
    D. Euphrates

15. In what Gospel is Satan called Beelzebub?
    A. Matthew
    B. Mark
    C. Luke
    D. John

16. What prophet was exiled to Babylon?
    A. Isaiah
    B. Jonah
    C. Jeremiah
    D. Ezekiel

17. When Jesus called in a loud voice, who came forth?
    A. John Mark
    B. John the Baptist
    C. Mary
    D. Lazarus

18. What was Sarai's name changed to?
    A. Rachel
    B. Miriam
    C. Sarah
    D. Elisheba

19. Who slept during a raging storm on the Sea of Galilee?
    A. Paul
    B. Timothy
    C. Jesus
    D. Jonah

20. Who had a wife named Judith?
    A. Esau
    B. Abner
    C. Jairus
    D. Jethro

21. What just and good king of Judah was assassinated by two of his own court officials?

    A. King Jehu
    B. King Joash
    C. King Jehoash
    D. King Josiah

22. What Egyptian woman married Joseph, according to the book of Genesis?

    A. Asenath
    B. Chloe
    C. Abigail
    D. Vashti

23. In one of his many miracles, how many pots of water did Jesus turn into wine?

    A. 2
    B. 6
    C. 77
    D. 144

24. Who referred to Mary as "the mother of my Lord"?

    A. Herod's daughter
    B. John the Baptist
    C. Elisabeth
    D. Zacharias

25. Who was a widow for approximately eighty-four years?

    A. Mary
    B. Lois
    C. Eunice
    D. Anna

58

Who Is God?

Twenty descriptions of God are scattered throughout the Bible in fifty-two places. In this challenging exercise, try to name the book of the Bible that mentions each description.

Give yourself 10 points for each book you name correctly out of fifty-two possible answers. If you can name twenty, you've done extremely well. More than half correct, or a score of 260 or better, is truly outstanding.

1. Omnipotent or all-powerful is mentioned in what three Bible books?

2. Eternal or lasting without end is mentioned in what three Bible books?

3. Infinite or having no boundaries or limits is mentioned in what four Bible books?

4. Self-sufficient or self-existent is mentioned in what three Bible books?

5. Omnipresent or present everywhere is mentioned in what Bible book?

6. Light is mentioned in what two Bible books?

7. Sovereign or exercising supreme, permanent authority is mentioned in what two Bible books?

8. Omniscient or all-knowing is mentioned in what two Bible books?

9. Unchanging is mentioned in what two Bible books?

10. Holy is mentioned in what two Bible books?

11. Wise is mentioned in what three Bible books?

12. Righteous or just is mentioned in what three Bible books?

13. True or the truth is mentioned in what four Bible books?

14. Faithful is mentioned in what two Bible books?

15. Gracious is mentioned in what three Bible books?

16. Good is mentioned in what three Bible books?

17. Merciful is mentioned in what four Bible books?

18. Spirit is mentioned in what Bible book?

19. Love is mentioned in what three Bible books?

20. Trinity or three in one is mentioned in what two Bible books?

SECTION 4

THE BONUS SECTION

The nearer I approach to the end of my pilgrimage, the clearer is the evidence of the divine origin of the Bible, and the grandeur and sublimity of God's remedy for fallen man are more appreciated, and the future is illumined with hope and joy.

Francis Bacon, English philosopher, scientist, lawyer, and father of the scientific method

59

The Sixty Hardest Questions

Give yourself 20 bonus points for each answer you get correct.

1. Name five of the seven people who lived to be over nine hundred years old.
2. Who was the first left-handed person mentioned in the Bible?
3. What man of the Old Testament captured thirty-one kings?
4. Who was the only woman to have her age of death listed in the Bible?
5. What man in Genesis lived to be less than 111 years old?
6. Name either of the two kings who were burned to death.
7. Name the three times God the Father spoke audibly while Jesus was on earth.
8. How many years older was Aaron than his brother Moses?
9. Who was the first man mentioned in the Bible as shaving?
10. Whose head was put on display in the temple of Dagon after his death?
11. What type of animal was the first used for an animal sacrifice?
12. Who was Ruth's first husband?
13. Sarah died how many years after giving birth to Isaac?
14. How old was Jairus's daughter when Jesus brought her back to life?

15. Although Cain was the Bible's first murderer, who was the second?

16. While leading the Israelites out of Egypt, Moses took along the bones of what man?

17. What man was responsible for building the first altar mentioned in the Bible?

18. Who became the first person to convert to Christianity in Europe?

19. Name one of the three books of the New Testament that does not include the word *amen*.

20. Who was the only man that the Bible states was placed in a coffin?

21. The wives of what three men were found at a well?

22. Although lawyers are mentioned in the Bible eight times, who was the only one mentioned by name?

23. Who reigned for fifty-five years, the longest reigning king in the Bible?

24. Who was the first person God killed for being wicked?

25. Name six of the eight weapons mentioned in the Bible that people used to fight each other.

26. Who was the first Christian martyr?

27. What king had the shortest reign at only seven days?

28. Who was the first woman the Bible mentions as singing?

29. Who was Paul's teacher?

30. What was the name of Jacob's daughter?

31. Who was the first judge of Israel?

32. Who was Herod's brother?

33. Before becoming a disciple of Jesus, Andrew was a disciple of what other man?

34. What group of people did not believe in angels or resurrection from the dead?

35. Who was Goliath's brother?

36. What was the first question God asked in the entire Bible?

37. In the list of unclean birds in the book of Leviticus, what is the largest bird listed?

38. Who was the first person to be called a Hebrew in the Bible?

39. The mother of John the Baptist, Elisabeth, was a direct descendent of what Genesis man?

40. What two women of the Bible died during childbirth?

41. What was the first color mentioned in the Bible?

42. Who was the first man in the Bible to prophesy?

43. Name the three people in the entire Bible whose names begin with the letter F.

44. God speaks for the vast majority of what Bible book?

45. After Eden, what is the second region mentioned in the Bible?

46. Who broke his neck falling backward off a chair after hearing bad news?

47. Name either of David's two sisters.

48. Levites could not serve in the tabernacle until they reached what age?

49. What king, when calling his people to repent, even had animals fast?

50. What book of the Bible references people riding on white donkeys?

51. Who was the first apostle to be martyred?

52. Who became the youngest biblical king at age seven?

53. King David was the great-grandson of what famous woman?

54. Who was told by God to select his men for battle by the way they drank water?

55. Name five of the six cities that had only two letters in their names.

56. What is the only miracle of Jesus that is mentioned in all four Gospels?

57. According to Luke 2:1, Jesus was born during the reign of what man who ordered a census?

58. Besides Jesus, what two men fasted for forty days?

59. Name eight of the ten instances in the Bible in which someone was raised from the dead.

60. Name the four times that Jesus used fish in his miracles.

Reading the Bible in One Year

Here is a precise schedule for reading the Bible in one year that offers easily digested chunks of God's Word for consistent study. You may start on any date.

Day 1—Genesis 1–3
Day 2—Genesis 4–8
Day 3—Genesis 9–13
Day 4—Genesis 14–17
Day 5—Genesis 18–20
Day 6—Genesis 21–23
Day 7—Genesis 24–26
Day 8—Genesis 27–29
Day 9—Genesis 30–32
Day 10—Genesis 33–35
Day 11—Genesis 36–38
Day 12—Genesis 39–41
Day 13—Genesis 42–44
Day 14—Genesis 45–47
Day 15—Genesis 48–50
Day 16—Exodus 1–3
Day 17—Exodus 4–6
Day 18—Exodus 7–9
Day 19—Exodus 10–12
Day 20—Exodus 13–16
Day 21—Exodus 17–20
Day 22—Exodus 21–23
Day 23—Exodus 24–27

Day 24—Exodus 28–31
Day 25—Exodus 32–34
Day 26—Exodus 35–37
Day 27—Exodus 38–40
Day 28—Leviticus 1–4
Day 29—Leviticus 5–7
Day 30—Leviticus 8–10
Day 31—Leviticus 11–13
Day 32—Leviticus 14–16
Day 33—Leviticus 17–19
Day 34—Leviticus 20–21
Day 35—Leviticus 22–23
Day 36—Leviticus 24–25
Day 37—Leviticus 26–27
Day 38—Numbers 1–2
Day 39—Numbers 3–4
Day 40—Numbers 5–6
Day 41—Numbers 7
Day 42—Numbers 8–10
Day 43—Numbers 11–13
Day 44—Numbers 14–15
Day 45—Numbers 16–18
Day 46—Numbers 19–22

Special References

Alphabetical List of Names of God

Advocate—1 John 2:1

Almighty—Revelation 1:8

Alpha and Omega—Revelation 1:8

Amen—Revelation 3:14

Anointed One—Psalm 2:2

Apostle—Hebrews 3:1

Author and finisher of our faith—Hebrews 12:2

Beginning and end—Revelation 21:6

Beginning of the creation of God—Revelation 3:14

Bishop of your souls—1 Peter 2:25

Branch—Zechariah 3:8

Bread of life—John 6:35, 48

Bridegroom—Matthew 9:15

Carpenter—Mark 6:3

Chief shepherd—1 Peter 5:4

The Christ—Matthew 1:16

Comforter—Jeremiah 8:18

Consolation of Israel—Luke 2:25

Corner stone—Ephesians 2:20

Dayspring—Luke 1:78

Day star—2 Peter 1:19

Deliverer—Romans 11:26

Desire of all nations—Haggai 2:7

Door of the sheep—John 10:7

Emmanuel—Matthew 1:23

Everlasting Father—Isaiah 9:6

Faithful and true witness—Revelation 3:14

Firstfruits—1 Corinthians 15:23

Foundation—Isaiah 28:16

Fountain—Zechariah 13:1

Friend of publicans and sinners—Matthew 11:19

God—John 1:1

Good shepherd—John 10:11

Governor—Matthew 2:6

Great shepherd—Hebrews 13:20

Guide—Psalm 48:14

Head of the body (church)—Colossians 1:18

High Priest—Hebrews 3:1; 4:15

Holy One of Israel—Isaiah 41:14

Horn of salvation—Luke 1:69

I Am—Exodus 3:14

Jehovah—Psalm 83:18

Jesus—Matthew 1:21

King of Israel—Matthew 27:42

King of Kings—1 Timothy 6:15; Revelation 19:16

Lamb of God—John 1:29

Last Adam—1 Corinthians 15:45

Life—John 11:25

Light of the world—John 8:12; 9:5

Lion of the tribe of Judah—Revelation 5:5

Lord of Lords—1 Timothy 6:15; Revelation 19:16

Master—Matthew 23:8

Mediator—1 Timothy 2:5

Messiah—John 1:41

Mighty God—Isaiah 9:6

Morning star—Revelation 22:16

Nazarene—Matthew 2:23

Our passover—1 Corinthians 5:7

Potentate—1 Timothy 6:15

Prince of Peace—Isaiah 9:6

Prophet—Acts 3:22

Propitiation—1 John 2:2

Purifier—Malachi 3:3

Rabbi—John 1:49

Ransom—1 Timothy 2:6

Redeemer—Isaiah 41:14

Refiner—Malachi 3:3

Refuge—Isaiah 25:4

Resurrection—John 11:25

Righteousness—Jeremiah 23:6

Rock—Deuteronomy 32:4; 2 Samuel 22:47

Root and the offspring of David—Revelation 22:16

Rose of Sharon—Song of Solomon 2:1

Sacrifice—Ephesians 5:2

Saviour—Luke 1:47

Seed of David—2 Timothy 2:8

Seed of the woman—Genesis 3:15

Servant—Isaiah 42:1

Shepherd—1 Peter 2:25

Shiloh—Genesis 49:10

Son of David—Matthew 15:22

Son of God—Luke 1:35

Son of man—Matthew 18:11

Son of Mary—Mark 6:3

Son of the Most High—Luke 1:32

Stone—Isaiah 28:16

Sun of righteousness—Malachi 4:2

Teacher—Matthew 26:18

Truth—John 14:6

Vine—John 15:1

Way—John 14:6

Wonderful Counselor—Isaiah 9:6

Word—John 1:1

The Ten Commandments

1. Thou shalt have no other gods before me. (Exodus 20:3)

2. Thou shalt not make unto thee any graven image, or any likeness of any thing that is in heaven above, or that is in the earth beneath, or that is in the water under the earth. (Exodus 20:4)

3. Thou shalt not take the name of the LORD thy God in vain; for the LORD will not hold him guiltless that taketh his name in vain. (Exodus 20:7)

4. Remember the sabbath day, to keep it holy. (Exodus 20:8)

5. Honour thy father and thy mother: that thy days may be long upon the land which the LORD thy God giveth thee. (Exodus 20:12)

6. Thou shalt not kill. (Exodus 20:13)

7. Thou shalt not commit adultery. (Exodus 20:14)

8. Thou shalt not steal. (Exodus 20:15)

9. Thou shalt not bear false witness against thy neighbour. (Exodus 20:16)

10. Thou shalt not covet thy neighbour's house, thou shalt not covet thy neighbour's wife, nor his manservant, nor his maidservant, nor his ox, nor his ass, nor any thing that is thy neighbour's. (Exodus 20:17)

The Seven "I Am" Statements of Jesus

1. And Jesus said unto them, I am the bread of life. (John 6:35)

2. Then spake Jesus again unto them, saying, I am the light of the world. (John 8:12)

3. Then said Jesus unto them again, Verily, verily, I say unto you, I am the door of the sheep. (John 10:7).

4. I am the good shepherd: the good shepherd giveth his life for the sheep. (John 10:11)

5. Jesus said unto her, I am the resurrection, and the life. (John 11:25)

6. Jesus saith unto him, I am the way, the truth, and the life: no man cometh unto the Father, but by me. (John 14:6)

7. I am the true vine, and my Father is the husbandman. (John 15:1)

The Eight Beatitudes

1. Blessed are the poor in spirit: for theirs is the kingdom of heaven. (Matthew 5:3)

2. Blessed are they that mourn: for they shall be comforted. (Matthew 5:4)

3. Blessed are the meek: for they shall inherit the earth. (Matthew 5:5)

4. Blessed are they which do hunger and thirst after righteousness: for they shall be filled. (Matthew 5:6)

5. Blessed are the merciful: for they shall obtain mercy. (Matthew 5:7)

6. Blessed are the pure in heart: for they shall see God. (Matthew 5:8)

7. Blessed are the peacemakers: for they shall be called the children of God. (Matthew 5:9)

8. Blessed are they which are persecuted for righteousness' sake: for theirs is the kingdom of heaven. (Matthew 5:10)

Scripture Is Inspired by God

1. All Scripture is given by inspiration of God, and is profitable for doctrine, for reproof, for correction, for instruction in righteousness, that the man of God may be perfect, thoroughly furnished unto all good works. (2 Timothy 3:16–17)

2. Knowing this first, that no prophecy of Scripture is of any private interpretation. For the prophecy came not in old time by the will of man: but holy men of God spake as they were moved by the Holy Ghost. (2 Peter 1:20–21)

The Twenty-Four Titles of Christ

1. Adam, last Adam (1 Corinthians 15:45)

2. Alpha and Omega (Revelation 21:6)

3. Bread of life (John 6:35)

4. Chief corner stone (Ephesians 2:20)

5. Chief shepherd (1 Peter 5:4)

6. Emmanuel, God with us (Matthew 1:23)

7. Firstborn from the dead (Colossians 1:18)

8. Good shepherd (John 10:11)

9. Great shepherd of the sheep (Hebrews 13:20)

10. High Priest (Hebrews 3:1)

11. Holy One of God (Mark 1:24)

12. King of Kings, Lord of Lords (Revelation 19:16)

13. Lamb of God (John 1:29)

14. Light of the world (John 9:5)

15. Lion of Judah (Revelation 5:5)

16. Lord of glory (1 Corinthians 2:8)

17. Mediator between God and men (1 Timothy 2:5)

18. Only begotten of the Father (John 1:14)

19. Prophet (Acts 3:22)

20. Saviour (Luke 1:47)

21. Seed of Abraham (Galatians 3:16)

22. Son of God (Mark 1:1)

23. Son of man (Matthew 18:11)

24. The Word (John 1:1)

The Twelve Apostles

1. Simon Peter

2. Andrew (Peter's brother)

3. James (son of Zebedee)

4. John (James's brother)

5. Philip

   6. Bartholomew

   7. Thomas

   8. Matthew

   9. James (son of Alphaeus)

   10. Thaddaeus

   11. Simon

   12. Judas Iscariot (After Judas betrayed the Lord Jesus
       Christ, Matthias was chosen by the other disciples as his
       replacement.)

Seven Women Who Had Miraculous Births

   1. Sarah, Abraham's wife (Genesis 11:30)

   2. Rebekah, Isaac's wife (Genesis 25:21)

   3. Rachel, Jacob's wife (Genesis 29:31)

   4. Samson's mother (Judges 13:2)

   5. Hannah, Samuel's mother (1 Samuel 1:5)

   6. Elisabeth, the mother of John the Baptist (Luke 1:7)

   7. Mary, the virgin mother of Jesus (Luke 1:26–2:20)

Ten People Who Were Raised from the Dead

   1. Widow of Zarephath's son, by Elijah (1 Kings 17:22)

   2. Shunammite woman's son, by Elisha (2 Kings 4:34–35)

   3. The man who came in contact with Elisha's bones
      (2 Kings 13:20–21)

   4. Widow of Nain's son, raised by Jesus (Luke 7:14–15)

   5. Jairus's daughter, raised by Jesus (Luke 8:52–56)

   6. Lazarus, raised by Jesus (John 11)

7. Jesus (Matthew 28:6; Acts 2:24)

8. The mass of holy people in tombs when Jesus gave up his spirit (Matthew 27:52–53)

9. Dorcas, by Peter (Acts 9:40)

10. Eutychus, by Paul (Acts 20:9–12)

Witnesses Who Saw Jesus Christ after His Resurrection

1. Mary Magdalene (Mark 16:9)

2. The other women (Matthew 28:9)

3. The two disciples (Luke 24:15)

4. The eleven disciples (Luke 24:36)

5. Peter (1 Corinthians 15:5)

6. Five hundred brethren (1 Corinthians 15:6)

7. Ten disciples (John 20:19)

8. James (1 Corinthians 15:7)

9. Witnesses at his ascension (Luke 24:50)

10. Paul (Acts 9:5; 1 Corinthians 15:8)

Score Card

	Possible Scores	Bonus Points	Your Scores
	4,002	1,225	
Section 1: The Must-Know Section			
2 150 Key Verses	300		
3 The Ten Plagues Inflicted on Egypt	280		
4 The Love of Money	6		
5 Being Truly Prosperous	28		
6 Being a Good Steward over One's Money	12		
7 Saving	10		
8 Tithing	34		
9 Ultimate Success	24		
Specialized Multiple-Choice Trivia			
11 Fly High	6		
12 What's That I Hear?	9		
13 The Story of Joseph	12		
14 Have a Laugh	10		
15 Anything Goes	50		
16 Priests	8		
17 Lions' Den	8		
18 More of Anything Goes	70		
Scripture Fill in the Blanks			
20 Scriptures on Hope	16		
21 Scriptures on Love	92		

	Possible Scores	Bonus Points	Your Scores
Section 2: The Advanced Section			
Specialized True or False Trivia			
22 Group 1	20		
23 Group 2	20		
24 Group 3	20		
25 Group 4	20		
26 Group 5	20		
27 Group 6	20		
28 Group 7	20		
29 Group 8	20		
30 Group 9	20		
31 Group 10	10		
Word Searches			
33 Women in the Bible Part 1	10		
34 Women in the Bible Part 2	10		
35 Women in the Bible Part 3	25		
36 Paul's Journeys Part 1	10		
37 Paul's Journeys Part 2	10		
38 Paul's Journeys Part 3	25		
39 Prisoners and Exiles Part 1	10		
40 Prisoners and Exiles Part 2	10		
41 Prisoners and Exiles Part 3	25		
43 Who Is?	100		
Section 3: The Bible Brilliant Section			
44 Crossword Puzzle		25	
Four Groups of Trivia			
45 Group 1	250		
46 Group 2	250		
47 Group 3	250		
48 Group 4	250		

	Possible Scores	Bonus Points	Your Scores
49 Fulfilled Prophecies about Jesus	720		
50 The Fast 100	100		
Trivia By Topic			
51 Who Asked?	24		
52 Hearing from God	16		
53 Bible Brilliant Level	40		
54 Anything Goes	92		
55 Royalty	20		
56 Firsts	20		
57 Random Bible Trivia	50		
58 Who Is God?	520		
Section 4: The Bonus Section			
59 The Sixty Hardest Questions		1,200	

Answers

SECTION 1: THE MUST-KNOW SECTION

---

2. 150 Key Verses

1. spirit
2. darkness
3. seventy
4. Pharisees
5. Elisabeth
6. Uzziah
7. throne
8. nature
9. repent
10. abomination
11. God
12. temple
13. save
14. Teaching
15. sepulchre
16. priest
17. name
18. God
19. gospel
20. Father
21. prison
22. times
23. fruit
24. gods
25. Peter
26. forgive
27. men
28. masters
29. heaven
30. Son
31. covenant
32. condemned
33. riches
34. name
35. sins
36. proud
37. tongues
38. heaven
39. firmament
40. John
41. temptation
42. enemies
43. end
44. written
45. wise
46. Satan
47. tooth
48. him
49. world
50. tempted
51. received
52. peace
53. light
54. soul
55. abominations
56. season
57. prophesy
58. Jerusalem
59. incense
60. equal
61. virgin
62. Rejoice
63. judge
64. bosom
65. law
66. love
67. scriptures
68. love
69. world
70. enemy
71. trump
72. cross
73. commandment
74. Timothy
75. tongues
76. Satan
77. tempted
78. Spirit
79. household
80. Antioch
81. perish
82. wrath
83. Christ
84. power
85. godliness
86. dead
87. Philip
88. bread
89. word
90. church
91. mother
92. Christ
93. Peter
94. repent
95. fire
96. David
97. world
98. pray
99. Blessed

100. ungodly
101. prophet
102. fear
103. servants
104. God
105. Israel
106. righteous
107. sabbath
108. unclean
109. sabbath
110. sixth
111. possessed
112. Jesus
113. Moses
114. fear
115. unbelieving
116. prophets
117. receive
118. save
119. Israel
120. kingdom
121. Blessed
122. faith
123. ask
124. seven
125. Mary
126. Father
127. five
128. ransom
129. masters
130. Ananias
131. Andrew
132. grudge
133. ghost
134. Salome
135. light
136. perfect
137. heaven
138. flesh
139. sword
140. knowledge
141. iniquity
142. rich
143. offspring
144. stewards
145. women
146. deceit
147. mind
148. parents
149. beginning
150. thoughts

3. The Ten Plagues Inflicted on Egypt

1.
   1. Water turned into blood

2.
   5. Death of livestock

3.
   9. Darkness

4.
   1. Water turned into blood
   4. Flies
   5. Death of livestock
   8. Locusts
   9. Darkness

5.
   2. Frogs
   3. Lice
   6. Boils
   7. Hailstorm

6.
   2. Frogs
   3. Lice
   4. Flies
   6. Boils
   7. Hailstorm
   9. Darkness

7.
   1. Water turned into blood
   2. Frogs
   3. Lice
   4. Flies
   5. Death of livestock
   6. Boils
   7. Hailstorm
   8. Locusts
   9. Darkness
   10. Death of all firstborn

4. The Love of Money

1. Mark 4:19
   And the cares of this <u>world</u>,
   and the deceitfulness of <u>riches</u>,
   and the lusts of other things
   entering in, <u>choke</u> the word, and
   it becometh <u>unfruitful</u>.

2. Mark 8:36
   For what shall it <u>profit</u> a man, if
   he shall gain the whole <u>world</u>,
   and <u>lose</u> his own <u>soul</u>?

3. 1 Timothy 6:9–11
   But they that will be rich fall into
   <u>temptation</u> and a snare, and
   into many foolish and hurtful
   <u>lusts</u>, which drown men in
   <u>destruction</u> and perdition. For
   the love of money is the root
   of all evil: which while some
   coveted after, they have erred
   from the faith, and pierced
   themselves through with many
   sorrows. But thou, O man of
   God, flee these things; and
   follow after <u>righteousness</u>,
   godliness, faith, love, <u>patience</u>,
   <u>meekness</u>.

5. Being Truly Prosperous

1. Genesis 26:12
   Then Isaac sowed in that <u>land</u>,
   and received in the same <u>year</u>
   an <u>hundredfold</u>: and the Lord
   <u>blessed</u> him.

2. Genesis 39:3
   And his <u>master</u> saw that the
   Lord was with him, and that the
   <u>Lord</u> made all that he did to
   <u>prosper</u> in his <u>hand</u>.

3. Deuteronomy 8:18
   But thou shalt <u>remember</u> the
   Lord thy God: for it is he that
   giveth thee <u>power</u> to get <u>wealth</u>,
   that he may establish his
   <u>covenant</u> which he sware unto
   thy <u>fathers</u>, as it is this day.

4. Deuteronomy 15:10
   <u>Thou</u> shalt surely give him, and
   thine heart shall not be <u>grieved</u>
   when thou givest unto him:
   because that for this thing the
   Lord thy God shall <u>bless</u> thee
   in all thy <u>works</u>, and in all that
   thou puttest thine <u>hand</u> unto.

5. Deuteronomy 24:19
   When thou cuttest down thine
   <u>harvest</u> in thy field, and hast
   forgot a <u>sheaf</u> in the field, thou
   shalt not go again to <u>fetch</u> it: it
   shall be for the stranger, for the
   fatherless, and for the widow:
   that the <u>Lord</u> thy God may bless
   thee in all the <u>work</u> of thine
   hands.

6. Deuteronomy 30:8–10
   And thou shalt return and obey
   the voice of the Lord, and do
   all his commandments which
   I command thee this day. And
   the Lord thy God will make thee
   plenteous in every <u>work</u> of thine
   hand, in the fruit of thy body,
   and in the fruit of thy <u>cattle</u>,
   and in the fruit of thy land, for
   good: for the Lord will again
   rejoice over thee for good, as
   he rejoiced over thy <u>fathers</u>:
   If thou shalt hearken unto the
   voice of the Lord thy God, to

keep his <u>commandments</u> and his statutes which are written in this book of the law, and if thou turn unto the Lord thy God with all thine heart, and with all thy <u>soul</u>.

7. Joshua 1:8
This book of the law shall not depart out of thy <u>mouth</u>; but thou shalt meditate therein day and <u>night</u>, that thou mayest observe to do according to all that is <u>written</u> therein: for then thou shalt make thy way prosperous, and then thou shalt have good <u>success</u>.

8. 1 Chronicles 22:12
Only the <u>Lord</u> give thee wisdom and understanding, and give thee <u>charge</u> concerning Israel, that thou mayest keep the <u>law</u> of the Lord thy God.

9. 2 Chronicles 31:20
And thus did <u>Hezekiah</u> throughout all <u>Judah</u>, and wrought that which was good and right and truth before the <u>Lord</u> his <u>God</u>.

10. Psalm 1:1–3
Blessed is the man that walketh not in the counsel of the <u>ungodly</u>, nor standeth in the way of sinners, nor sitteth in the seat of the <u>scornful</u>. But his delight is in the law of the Lord; and in his law doth he meditate day and night. And he shall be like a tree planted by the rivers of <u>water</u>, that bringeth

forth his fruit in his season; his leaf also shall not wither; and whatsoever he doeth shall <u>prosper</u>.

11. Psalm 35:27
Let them shout for joy, and be glad, that favour my <u>righteous</u> cause: yea, let them say continually, Let the Lord be <u>magnified</u>, which hath pleasure in the <u>prosperity</u> of his <u>servant</u>.

12. Jeremiah 17:8
For he shall be as a tree planted by the <u>waters</u>, and that spreadeth out her roots by the <u>river</u>, and shall not see when heat cometh, but her leaf shall be <u>green</u>; and shall not be careful in the year of <u>drought</u>, neither shall cease from yielding fruit.

13. Malachi 3:10
Bring ye all the <u>tithes</u> into the storehouse, that there may be meat in mine <u>house</u>, and prove me now herewith, saith the <u>Lord</u> of <u>hosts</u>, if I will not open you the windows of <u>heaven</u>, and pour you out a <u>blessing</u>, that there shall not be room enough to receive it.

14. 3 John 1:2
<u>Beloved</u>, I wish above all things that thou mayest <u>prosper</u> and be in <u>health</u>, even as thy <u>soul</u> prospereth.

6. Being a Good Steward over One's Money

1. Genesis 2:15
   And the Lord God <u>took</u> the man, and put him into the <u>garden</u> of <u>Eden</u> to dress it and to <u>keep</u> it.

2. Deuteronomy 10:14
   <u>Behold</u>, the <u>heaven</u> and the heaven of <u>heavens</u> is the Lord's thy God, the <u>earth</u> also, with all that therein is.

3. Luke 12:42–44
   And the Lord said, Who then is that faithful and wise <u>steward</u>, whom his lord shall make <u>ruler</u> over his <u>household</u>, to give them their portion of <u>meat</u> in due season? Blessed is that <u>servant</u>, whom his lord when he cometh shall find so doing. Of a truth I say unto you, that he will make him ruler over all that he hath.

4. Luke 12:47–48
   And that <u>servant</u>, which knew his lord's will, and prepared not himself, neither did according to his will, shall be beaten with many stripes. But he that knew not, and did commit things worthy of <u>stripes</u>, shall be beaten with few stripes. For unto <u>whomsoever</u> much is given, of him shall be much required: and to whom men have <u>committed</u> much, of him they will ask the more.

5. Luke 16:9–11
   And I say unto you, Make to yourselves <u>friends</u> of the mammon of unrighteousness; that, when ye fail, they may receive you into everlasting habitations. He that is faithful in that which is least is <u>faithful</u> also in much: and he that is unjust in the least is <u>unjust</u> also in much. If therefore ye have not been faithful in the unrighteous <u>mammon</u>, who will commit to your trust the true <u>riches</u>?

6. Romans 14:8
   For whether we live, we live unto the Lord; and whether we <u>die</u>, we die unto the <u>Lord</u>: whether we <u>live</u> therefore, or die, we are the <u>Lord's</u>.

7. Saving

1. Proverbs 21:5
   The <u>thoughts</u> of the diligent <u>tend</u> only to plenteousness; but of every one that is <u>hasty</u> only to <u>want</u>.

2. Proverbs 21:20
   There is <u>treasure</u> to be desired and <u>oil</u> in the dwelling of the <u>wise</u>; but a foolish man <u>spendeth</u> it up.

3. Proverbs 27:12
   A <u>prudent</u> man foreseeth the <u>evil</u>, and hideth himself; but the <u>simple</u> pass on, and are <u>punished</u>.

4. Proverbs 30:25
   The ants are a <u>people</u> not strong, yet they prepare their meat in the <u>summer</u>.

5. 1 Corinthians 16:2
   Upon the first <u>day</u> of the <u>week</u> let every one of you lay by him in store, as <u>God</u> hath prospered him, that there be no <u>gatherings</u> when I come.

8. Tithing

1. Genesis 14:20
   And blessed be the most high <u>God</u>, which hath delivered <u>thine</u> enemies into thy <u>hand</u>. And he gave him <u>tithes</u> of all.

2. Genesis 28:20–22
   And <u>Jacob</u> vowed a vow, saying, If God will be with me, and will keep me in this way that I go, and will give me <u>bread</u> to eat, and raiment to put on, So that I come again to my father's <u>house</u> in peace; then shall the Lord be my God: And this stone, which I have set for a <u>pillar</u>, shall be God's house: and of all that thou shalt give me I will surely give the <u>tenth</u> unto thee.

3. Exodus 23:19
   The first of the <u>firstfruits</u> of thy <u>land</u> thou shalt bring into the <u>house</u> of the Lord thy God. Thou shalt not seethe a <u>kid</u> in his mother's <u>milk</u>.

4. Leviticus 27:30
   And all the <u>tithe</u> of the <u>land</u>, whether of the <u>seed</u> of the land, or of the fruit of the tree, is the Lord's: it is holy unto the <u>Lord</u>.

5. Numbers 18:26
   Thus speak unto the <u>Levites</u>, and say unto them, When ye take of the children of <u>Israel</u> the tithes which I have given you from them for your <u>inheritance</u>, then ye shall offer up an heave offering of it for the Lord, even a tenth part of the <u>tithe</u>.

6. Deuteronomy 14:22–23
   Thou shalt truly <u>tithe</u> all the increase of thy seed, that the field bringeth forth <u>year</u> by year. And thou shalt eat before the Lord thy God, in the place which he shall choose to place his <u>name</u> there, the tithe of thy <u>corn</u>, of thy wine, and of thine oil, and the <u>firstlings</u> of thy herds and of thy <u>flocks</u>; that thou mayest learn to fear the Lord thy God always.

7. Deuteronomy 14:28
   At the end of <u>three</u> years thou shalt bring forth all the tithe of thine <u>increase</u> the same <u>year</u>, and shalt lay it up within thy <u>gates</u>.

8. Deuteronomy 26:12
   When thou hast made an end of <u>tithing</u> all the tithes of thine increase the third year, which is the year of tithing, and hast given it unto the <u>Levite</u>, the <u>stranger</u>, the <u>fatherless</u>, and the <u>widow</u>, that they may eat within thy gates, and be filled.

9. 2 Chronicles 31:5
   And as soon as the <u>commandment</u> came abroad, the children of <u>Israel</u> brought in abundance the firstfruits of corn, <u>wine</u>, and oil, and honey, and of all the increase of the field; and the <u>tithe</u> of all things brought they in <u>abundantly</u>.

10. Nehemiah 10:38
    And the priest the son of <u>Aaron</u> shall be with the <u>Levites</u>, when the Levites take <u>tithes</u>: and the Levites shall bring up the tithe of the tithes unto the <u>house</u> of our God, to the chambers, into the <u>treasure</u> house.

11. Proverbs 3:9–10
    Honour the <u>Lord</u> with thy substance, and with the firstfruits of all thine increase: So shall thy <u>barns</u> be filled with plenty, and thy presses shall burst out with new <u>wine</u>.

12. Ezekiel 44:30
    And the first of all the <u>firstfruits</u> of all things, and every oblation of all, of every sort of your oblations, shall be the priest's: ye shall also give unto the <u>priest</u> the first of your <u>dough</u>, that he may cause the <u>blessing</u> to rest in thine house.

13. Amos 4:4
    Come to <u>Bethel</u>, and transgress; at Gilgal multiply <u>transgression</u>; and bring your <u>sacrifices</u> every morning, and your <u>tithes</u> after three years.

14. Malachi 3:8
    Will a man <u>rob</u> God? Yet ye have <u>robbed</u> me. But ye say, Wherein have we robbed <u>thee</u>? In <u>tithes</u> and <u>offerings</u>.

15. Matthew 23:23
    Woe unto you, scribes and <u>Pharisees</u>, hypocrites! for ye pay tithe of mint and anise and <u>cummin</u>, and have omitted the <u>weightier</u> matters of the law, <u>judgment</u>, mercy, and faith: these ought ye to have done, and not to leave the other <u>undone</u>.

16. 1 Corinthians 16:1–2
    Now concerning the collection for the <u>saints</u>, as I have given order to the <u>churches</u> of <u>Galatia</u>, even so do ye. Upon the first day of the <u>week</u> let every one of you lay by him in store, as <u>God</u> hath prospered him, that there be no gatherings when I come.

17. Hebrews 7:4
    Now consider how great this <u>man</u> was, unto whom even the <u>patriarch</u> Abraham gave the tenth of the <u>spoils</u>.

9. Ultimate Success

1. Deuteronomy 30:9
   And the Lord thy God will make thee plenteous in every work of thine <u>hand</u>, in the fruit of thy body, and in the <u>fruit</u> of thy cattle, and in the fruit of thy land, for good: for the Lord will again <u>rejoice</u> over thee for good, as he rejoiced over thy <u>fathers</u>.

2. Joshua 1:8
   This book of the law shall not depart out of thy <u>mouth</u>; but thou shalt <u>meditate</u> therein day and <u>night</u>, that thou mayest observe to do according to all that is written therein: for then thou shalt make thy way <u>prosperous</u>, and then thou shalt have good <u>success</u>.

3. Nehemiah 2:20
   Then <u>answered</u> I them, and said unto them, The God of <u>heaven</u>, he will prosper us; therefore we his servants will arise and <u>build</u>: but ye have no <u>portion</u>, nor right, nor memorial, in Jerusalem.

4. Psalm 1:1–3

Blessed is the man that <u>walketh</u> not in the counsel of the ungodly, nor standeth in the way of sinners, nor sitteth in the seat of the scornful. But his <u>delight</u> is in the law of the Lord; and in his law doth he <u>meditate</u> day and night. And he shall be like a tree planted by the <u>rivers</u> of water, that bringeth forth his fruit in his season; his leaf also shall not <u>wither</u>; and whatsoever he doeth shall <u>prosper</u>.

5. Psalm 37:4

Delight <u>thyself</u> also in the <u>Lord</u>: and he shall give thee the <u>desires</u> of thine <u>heart</u>.

6. Proverbs 22:29

Seest thou a man diligent in his <u>business</u>? he shall stand before <u>kings</u>; he shall not stand before mean <u>men</u>.

7. Proverbs 22:4

By <u>humility</u> and the <u>fear</u> of the Lord are <u>riches</u>, and honour, and <u>life</u>.

8. Isaiah 1:19

If ye be <u>willing</u> and <u>obedient</u>, ye shall eat the <u>good</u> of the <u>land</u>.

9. Matthew 6:24

No man can <u>serve</u> two <u>masters</u>: for either he will hate the one, and <u>love</u> the other; or else he will hold to the one, and <u>despise</u> the other. Ye cannot serve God and <u>mammon</u>.

10. Matthew 23:12

And <u>whosoever</u> shall exalt himself shall be <u>abased</u>; and he that shall humble himself shall be <u>exalted</u>.

11. Luke 9:48

And said unto them, <u>Whosoever</u> shall receive this child in my <u>name</u> receiveth me: and whosoever shall receive me receiveth him that sent me: for he that is least among <u>you</u> all, the same shall be <u>great</u>.

12. Ephesians 3:20

Now unto him that is able to do exceeding abundantly above all that we <u>ask</u> or <u>think</u>, according to the <u>power</u> that <u>worketh</u> in us.

11. Fly High

1. B (James 3:7–8)
2. C (Matthew 3:16)
3. D (Genesis 7:2–3)
4. A (Revelation 1:1–2; 12:14)
5. B (Exodus 16:13)
6. C (Mark 4:1–4)

12. What's That I Hear?

1. A (Acts 2:1–14)
2. A (Revelation 1:1–2; 18:1–3)
3. B (Matthew 3:16–17)
4. C (Revelation 1:1–2; 6:10)
5. C (1 Kings 19:1–21)
6. D (1 Samuel 3:2–4)
7. C (Psalm 29:5)
8. D (2 Kings 19:14–22)
9. C (1 Samuel 28:7–12)

13. The Story of Joseph

1. B (Genesis 42:3)
2. B (Genesis 42:4)
3. A (Genesis 42:17)
4. D (Genesis 42:18–24)
5. A (Genesis 42:25)
6. B (Genesis 44:2)
7. C (Genesis 44:17)
8. B (Genesis 47:1–6)
9. B (Genesis 45:18)
10. C (Genesis 50:26)
11. D (Genesis 41:51)
12. C (Genesis 45:22)

14. Have a Laugh

1. B (Matthew 9:23–24)
2. C (Genesis 17:17)
3. A (2 Samuel 6:12–14)
4. D (Genesis 18:12)
5. A (Exodus 32:4, 19)
6. D (Genesis 21:6)
7. C (Luke 6:21)
8. D (Judges 11:34)
9. C (1 Samuel 30:16–19)
10. A (Nehemiah 2:19)

15. Anything Goes

1. C (Matthew 4:7)
2. D (Matthew 2:14)
3. C (Matthew 8:14)
4. B (Numbers 11:28)
5. D (Proverbs 31:10)
6. B (Matthew 26:65)
7. A (Esther 8:2)
8. C (1 Samuel 17:26–28)
9. A (2 Kings 11:2–3)
10. A (Ruth 1:20)
11. B (Revelation 1:9)
12. D (Acts 18:1–3)
13. B (Jonah 1:15)
14. C (Job 42:12–14)
15. C (Acts 6:8–9; 7:59–60; 8:1)
16. B (Genesis 41:50–52)
17. C (2 Kings 15:29)
18. B (John 9:6)
19. B (Genesis 42:29–32; 48:10)
20. D (Mark 10:46–52)
21. B (Jonah 3:1–10)
22. C (Acts 18:24–26)
23. C (2 Chronicles 30:1–10)
24. A (1 Kings 15:17)
25. B (2 Kings 21:18–19, 23)
26. A (1 Samuel 22:1–2; 23:14–29)
27. D (John 13:6–8)
28. B (Galatians 1:19)
29. B (Exodus 7:1; 32:15–24)
30. D (2 Samuel 4:4)
31. A (2 Kings 6:24–30)
32. C (Luke 2:36–38)
33. C (John 4:7–15)
34. B (Genesis 12:14–19)
35. A (Deuteronomy 3:11)
36. D (Joshua 9:7–27)
37. C (2 Corinthians 11:13–14)
38. D (1 Samuel 22:13–17)
39. B (John 20:1–2)
40. D (1 Samuel 18:1–30)
41. B (Habakkuk 1:1; 2:6)
42. D (Mark 12:1–12)
43. C (2 Chronicles 21:1–6)
44. B (Matthew 25:14–30)
45. D (Joshua 6:22–25)
46. B (2 Samuel 13:1–36)
47. A (2 Kings 11:21; 12:1–3)
48. C (Zechariah 1:1–2; 2:1–3)
49. D (2 Kings 3:4)
50. C 27

16. Priests

1. C (Deuteronomy 17:12)
2. B (Exodus 28:15–21)
3. B (Hebrews 7:1–3)
4. B (Hebrews 7:1–3)
5. A (1 Samuel 1:12–14)
6. D (2 Kings 23:1–30)
7. C (1 Samuel 2:12–17, 34)
8. B (Exodus 18:13–27)

17. Lions' Den

1. C (Revelation 1:1–2; 4:6–7)
2. D (Daniel 7:2–4)
3. C (1 Samuel 17:34–35)
4. A (1 Peter 5:8)
5. B (Judges 14:5–6)
6. B (2 Samuel 1:23)
7. C (Ezekiel 1:1–10)
8. D (2 Samuel 23:20)

18. More of Anything Goes

1. B (Numbers 8:5–7)
2. D (Judges 7:13)
3. A (Genesis 20:2)
4. B (2 Kings 9:22)
5. D (Matthew 26:6)
6. B (Song of Solomon 1:1)
7. A (Daniel 5:31)
8. B (Ezekiel 23:2–4)
9. A (2 Kings 17:27)
10. A (John 20:2–4)
11. C (Isaiah 8:1–4)
12. B (1 Kings 16:8–10)
13. B (1 Kings 2:20)
14. B (Judges 21:20–21)
15. C (Job 8:1, 20–21)
16. A (Numbers 21:1)
17. C (Isaiah 1:1; 24:21–22)
18. B (Acts 9:36, 39)
19. A (Numbers 12:15)
20. A (1 Samuel 28:7–25)
21. B (1 Kings 17:9–15)
22. C (2 Kings 4:8–37; 8:1)
23. B (John 8:3–11)
24. A (Genesis 6:2)
25. B (John 11:1)
26. D (Matthew 26:3)
27. C (Deuteronomy 18:1–2)
28. D (Genesis 4:22)
29. C (Genesis 4:17)
30. B (Genesis 17:9–10)
31. D (John 4:46–54)
32. B (Acts 15:40)
33. A (Genesis 29:33)
34. C (2 Samuel 2:9–11)
35. B (Genesis 5:20)
36. D (Ezra 3:8–9; 5:2; 6:14–16)
37. D (Job 38:1)
38. C (2 Samuel 4:4)
39. A (2 Samuel 17:14, 23)
40. A (1 Samuel 17:5)
41. C (Malachi 3:8)
42. D (Jeremiah 39:1)
43. A (2 Kings 11:15–18)
44. D (Nehemiah 3:1)
45. C (Acts 2:14–17)
46. B (Romans 16:6)
47. C (Mark 6:22)
48. D (Hosea 1:1–2, 9)
49. B (1 Kings 1:5–11)
50. B (Judges 4:1–3)
51. A (1 Kings 11:19)
52. C (Luke 17:11–19)
53. C (John 11:41–51)
54. C (Judges 3:17–22)
55. D (John 4:7, 17–18)
56. C (Acts 16:14)
57. D (Revelation 2:18–20)
58. B (1 Kings 14:2)
59. B (Acts 3:1; 4:3)
60. A (Genesis 31:24)

61. B (1 Kings 16:29–33)
62. A (Esther 2:1–18)
63. D (Matthew 24:1–2)
64. C (Exodus 17:15)
65. D (Amos 3:14)

66. B (2 Kings 15:13–15)
67. C (Acts 3:1; 4:1–4)
68. A (Acts 17:15–22)
69. D (Genesis 19:30)
70. D (Matthew)

20. Scriptures on Hope

1. Numbers 23:19
God is not a <u>man</u>, that he should <u>lie</u>; neither the son of man, that he should repent: hath he said, and shall he not do it? or hath he spoken, and shall he not make it <u>good</u>?

2. Job 13:15
Though he <u>slay</u> me, yet will I <u>trust</u> in him: but I will maintain mine own <u>ways</u> before him.

3. Proverbs 24:14
So shall the knowledge of <u>wisdom</u> be unto thy <u>soul</u>: when thou hast found it, then there shall be a reward, and thy <u>expectation</u> shall not be cut off.

4. Proverbs 24:20
For there shall be no reward to the <u>evil</u> man; the candle of the <u>wicked</u> shall be put out.

5. Romans 8:24–25
For we are saved by <u>hope</u>: but hope that is seen is not <u>hope</u>: for what a man seeth, why doth he yet hope for? But if we hope for that we see not, then do we with <u>patience</u> wait for it.

6. 1 Corinthians 15:19
If in this <u>life</u> only we have hope in <u>Christ</u>, we are of all men most <u>miserable</u>.

7. Hebrews 11:1
Now <u>faith</u> is the substance of things <u>hoped</u> for, the evidence of <u>things</u> not seen.

8. 1 Peter 1:3
Blessed be the <u>God</u> and Father of our Lord Jesus <u>Christ</u>, which according to his abundant mercy hath begotten us again unto a lively hope by the <u>resurrection</u> of Jesus Christ from the <u>dead</u>.

21. Scriptures on Love

1. Leviticus 19:17–18
Thou shalt not hate thy <u>brother</u> in thine heart: thou shalt in any wise rebuke thy neighbour, and not suffer <u>sin</u> upon him. Thou shalt not avenge, nor bear any grudge against the <u>children</u> of thy people, but thou shalt <u>love</u> thy neighbour as thyself: I am the Lord.

2. Psalm 30:5
For his <u>anger</u> endureth but a moment; in his favour is <u>life</u>: weeping may endure for a <u>night</u>, but joy cometh in the morning.

3. Psalm 103:8
The <u>Lord</u> is merciful and <u>gracious</u>, slow to anger, and plenteous in <u>mercy</u>.

4. Psalm 103:13

Like as a <u>father</u> pitieth his <u>children</u>, so the Lord pitieth them that fear <u>him</u>.

5. Psalm 143:8

Cause me to hear thy lovingkindness in the <u>morning</u>; for in thee do I trust: cause me to know the way wherein I should <u>walk</u>; for I lift up my soul unto thee.

6. Proverbs 10:12

<u>Hatred</u> stirreth up strifes: but <u>love</u> covereth all sins.

7. Proverbs 21:21

He that followeth after <u>righteousness</u> and mercy findeth <u>life</u>, righteousness, and honour.

8. Isaiah 43:4

Since thou wast precious in my <u>sight</u>, thou hast been honourable, and I have loved <u>thee</u>: therefore will I give men for thee, and people for thy <u>life</u>.

9. Matthew 5:44

But I say unto you, <u>Love</u> your <u>enemies</u>, bless them that curse you, do good to them that hate you, and pray for them which despitefully use you, and persecute <u>you</u>.

10. Mark 12:30

And thou shalt <u>love</u> the Lord thy God with all thy <u>heart</u>, and with all thy soul, and with all thy mind, and with all thy strength: this is the first <u>commandment</u>.

11. Mark 12:31

And the second is like, namely this, Thou shalt <u>love</u> thy neighbour as thyself. There is none other <u>commandment</u> greater than these.

12. Luke 10:27

And he answering said, <u>Thou</u> shalt love the Lord thy God with all thy <u>heart</u>, and with all thy <u>soul</u>, and with all thy strength, and with all thy mind; and thy neighbour as thyself.

13. John 14:21

He that hath my <u>commandments</u>, and keepeth them, he it is that <u>loveth</u> me: and he that loveth me shall be loved of my <u>Father</u>, and I will love him, and will manifest myself to him.

14. John 15:12

This is my <u>commandment</u>, That ye <u>love</u> one another, as I have <u>loved</u> you.

15. John 15:13

Greater love hath no <u>man</u> than this, that a man lay down his <u>life</u> for his <u>friends</u>.

16. Romans 8:38–39

For I am <u>persuaded</u>, that neither death, nor life, nor angels, nor principalities, nor <u>powers</u>, nor things present, nor things to come, nor <u>height</u>, nor depth, nor any other creature, shall be able to separate us from the love of <u>God</u>, which is in Christ Jesus our Lord.

17. Romans 12:9

Let <u>love</u> be without dissimulation. Abhor that which is <u>evil</u>; cleave to that which is good.

18. Romans 12:10
Be kindly affectioned one to another with brotherly <u>love</u>; in honour preferring one another.

19. Romans 13:8
Owe no man any thing, but to <u>love</u> one another: for he that loveth another hath fulfilled the <u>law</u>.

20. Romans 13:10
<u>Love</u> worketh no <u>ill</u> to his neighbour: therefore love is the fulfilling of the law.

21. 1 Corinthians 2:9
But as it is <u>written</u>, Eye hath not seen, nor ear <u>heard</u>, neither have entered into the heart of man, the things which God hath prepared for them that <u>love</u> him.

22. 1 Corinthians 10:24
Let no <u>man</u> seek his own, but every man another's <u>wealth</u>.

23. 1 Corinthians 13:1
Though I speak with the <u>tongues</u> of men and of <u>angels</u>, and have not charity, I am become as sounding brass, or a tinkling <u>cymbal</u>.

24. 1 Corinthians 13:2
And though I have the gift of <u>prophecy</u>, and understand all <u>mysteries</u>, and all knowledge; and though I have all faith, so that I could remove <u>mountains</u>, and have not charity, I am nothing.

25. 1 Corinthians 13:3
And though I bestow all my <u>goods</u> to feed the poor, and though I give my <u>body</u> to be burned, and have not charity, it profiteth me <u>nothing</u>.

26. 1 Corinthians 13:4–5
<u>Charity</u> suffereth long, and is kind; charity envieth not; charity vaunteth not itself, is not puffed up, doth not <u>behave</u> itself unseemly, seeketh not her own, is not easily provoked, thinketh no <u>evil</u>.

27. 1 Corinthians 16:14
Let all your <u>things</u> be done with <u>charity</u>.

28. Ephesians 3:16–17
That he would grant you, according to the <u>riches</u> of his <u>glory</u>, to be strengthened with might by his <u>Spirit</u> in the inner man; that Christ may dwell in your hearts by faith; that ye, being rooted and grounded in <u>love</u>.

29. Ephesians 4:2
With all lowliness and <u>meekness</u>, with longsuffering, forbearing one another in <u>love</u>.

30. Ephesians 4:15
But speaking the truth in <u>love</u>, may grow up into him in all <u>things</u>, which is the head, even <u>Christ</u>.

31. Ephesians 5:2
And walk in love, as Christ also hath <u>loved</u> us, and hath given <u>himself</u> for us an offering and a sacrifice to <u>God</u> for a sweetsmelling savour.

32. Ephesians 5:25–26
<u>Husbands</u>, love your <u>wives</u>, even as Christ also loved the church, and gave himself for it; That

he might sanctify and cleanse
it with the washing of water by
the word.

33. Colossians 3:14

And above all these things put
on <u>charity</u>, which is the bond of
<u>perfectness</u>.

34. 1 Thessalonians 3:12

And the Lord make you to
increase and abound in <u>love</u>
one toward another, and toward
all <u>men</u>, even as we do toward
you.

35. 2 Thessalonians 3:5

And the Lord direct your <u>hearts</u>
into the love of God, and into
the <u>patient</u> waiting for Christ.

36. 2 Timothy 1:7

For God hath not given us the
spirit of <u>fear</u>; but of power, and
of love, and of a sound <u>mind</u>.

37. 1 Peter 4:8

And above all things have
fervent <u>charity</u> among
yourselves: for charity shall
cover the multitude of <u>sins</u>.

38. 1 John 3:1

Behold, what manner of love
the <u>Father</u> hath bestowed upon
<u>us</u>, that we should be called
the sons of God: therefore the
world knoweth us not, because
it knew him not.

39. 1 John 3:11

For this is the message that ye
heard from the <u>beginning</u>, that
we should <u>love</u> one another.

40. 1 John 4:9

In this was manifested the <u>love</u>
of God toward us, because that
God sent his only begotten Son

into the <u>world</u>, that we might
live through him.

41. 1 John 4:10

Herein is <u>love</u>, not that we
loved God, but that he loved
us, and sent his <u>Son</u> to be the
propitiation for our <u>sins</u>.

42. 1 John 4:12

No man hath seen <u>God</u> at any
time. If we love one another,
God dwelleth in us, and his love
is perfected in <u>us</u>.

43. 1 John 4:16

And we have known and
believed the <u>love</u> that God hath
to us. God is <u>love</u>; and he that
dwelleth in love dwelleth in God,
and God in him.

44. 1 John 4:18

There is no fear in love; but
perfect <u>love</u> casteth out <u>fear</u>:
because fear hath torment. He
that feareth is not made perfect
in <u>love</u>.

45. 1 John 4:20

If a man say, I love God, and
hateth his brother, he is a
<u>liar</u>: for he that loveth not his
<u>brother</u> whom he hath seen,
how can he love God whom he
hath not seen?

46. Revelation 3:19

As many as I <u>love</u>, I rebuke and
<u>chasten</u>: be zealous therefore,
and repent.

SECTION 2: THE ADVANCED SECTION

22. Group 1

1. True—(John 4:6–19)
2. False—He asked for a drink of water (John 4:7)
3. True—(John 6:1)
4. False—Judas Iscariot betrayed him with a kiss (Mark 14:43–45; John 6:70–71)
5. True—(John 8:44)
6. False—Jonah asked to be cast into the sea (Jonah 1:12)
7. False—He was in the fish for three days and three nights (Jonah 1:17)
8. True—(Jonah 1:3)
9. False—He prayed (Jonah 2:1)
10. False—It would be overturned in forty days (Jonah 3:4)
11. False—He was Joshua's father (Joshua 1:1)
12. True—(Joshua 1:4)
13. True—(Joshua 2:1)
14. False—He was 110 years old when he died (Joshua 24:29)
15. True—(Joshua 24:32)
16. True—(Joshua 3:1–6)
17. True—(Joshua 6:20)
18. True—(Judges 11:3)
19. False—He had forty sons (Judges 12:13–14)
20. False—Manoah was his father (Judges 13:22–24)

23. Group 2

1. True—(Judges 14:5–9)
2. True—(Judges 16:15–20)
3. False—Samson was buried with his father, Manoah (Judges 16:31)
4. False—Micah stole the silver (Judges 17:1–2)
5. True—(Judges 17:5)
6. False—He was a very overweight man (Judges 3:17)
7. True—(Judges 3:17–21)
8. False—She gave the captain milk (Judges 4:19–21)
9. False—He was the king of Canaan (Judges 4:2)
10. False—Sisera was killed (Judges 4:21)
11. False—Israel was judged by Deborah (Judges 4:4)
12. False—Gideon was commissioned by an angel (Judges 6:11–23)
13. False—They attacked a Midianite camp late at night (Judges 7:19)
14. False—He was murdered by Gideon's army (Judges 7:25)
15. False—He defeated them with only three hundred men (Judges 7:7)
16. True—(Judges 8:26)
17. False—They experienced forty years of peace (Judges 8:28)
18. True—(Judges 8:30)

19. False—Camels were forbidden as food (Leviticus 11:4)

20. False—They had to cover the lower part of their face (Leviticus 13:45)

24. Group 3

1. False—A goat was released (Leviticus 16:22)
2. False—He anointed Aaron and his sons (Leviticus 8:23–30)
3. False—They were the sons of Aaron (Leviticus 10:1)
4. True—(Luke 1:22)
5. False—She was engaged (Luke 1:27)
6. True—(Luke 1:30–31)
7. True—(Luke 10:17–18)
8. True—(Luke 11:34)
9. False—A repentant sinner causes them to rejoice (Luke 15:10)
10. True—(Luke 17:12–16)
11. True—(Luke 17:18)
12. True—(Luke 19:2–4)
13. True—(Luke 19:8)
14. False—They saw him in Jerusalem at the temple (Luke 2:25, 27, 36–37)
15. True—(Luke 2:4)
16. True—(Luke 2:41)
17. True—(Luke 2:49)
18. True—(Luke 2:51)
19. False—He was born in a stable (Luke 2:7)
20. True—(Luke 22:19)

25. Group 4

1. True—(Luke 22:43)
2. True—(Luke 22:45)
3. True—(Luke 22:39)
4. True—(Luke 24:30)
5. False—He was governor of Judea (Luke 3:1)
6. True—(Luke 3:17)
7. False—The tax collector Levi held a feast for Jesus (Luke 5:29)
8. True—(Luke 5:29–32)
9. True—(Luke 5:8)
10. False—He said to bless them (Luke 6:20, 28)
11. True—(Luke 7:11–15)
12. False—Jesus was asleep on the boat (Luke 8:23–24)
13. False—He brought Jairus's daughter back to life (Luke 8:41–42, 49–55)
14. False—He sent Peter and John to prepare the meal (Luke 22:8)
15. False—He took the form of a dove (Mark 1:10)
16. False—He baptized them in the Jordan River (Mark 1:5)
17. False—John said he was unworthy (Mark 1:7)
18. True—(Mark 12:40)
19. True—(Mark 14:3)
20. True—(Mark 15:22)

26. Group 5

1. False—Two criminals were crucified with Jesus (Mark 15:22, 27)
2. True—(Mark 16:18)
3. False—Seven demons were cast out (Mark 16:9)
4. True—(Mark 16:9)
5. True—(Mark 3:17)
6. True—(Mark 6:56)
7. True—(Matthew 1:18–21)
8. False—It means "God with us" (Matthew 1:23)
9. True—(Matthew 1:3–17)
10. True—(Matthew 12:33)
11. False—He used five loaves of bread (Matthew 14:15–21)
12. False—Peter walked on water (Matthew 14:28–31)
13. False—She plotted the death of John the Baptist (Matthew 14:3–8)
14. False—He sent Peter (Matthew 17:24–27)
15. False—A star led them (Matthew 2:1–9)
16. False—They were in the east (Matthew 2:7–9)
17. True—(Matthew 21:14)
18. True—(Matthew 21:1–9)
19. True—(Matthew 24:3)
20. True—(Matthew 24–25)

27. Group 6

1. False—They are referred to as sheep (Matthew 25:31–34)
2. False—He was given thirty pieces of silver (Matthew 26:14–16)
3. True—(Matthew 26:14–16)
4. False—He denied Jesus three times (Matthew 26:34)
5. True—(Matthew 26:75)
6. True—(Matthew 27:26)
7. False—They were thieves (Matthew 27:44)
8. True—(Matthew 27:60)
9. False—It was known as "the field of blood" (Matthew 27:7–8)
10. True—(Matthew 3:1)
11. True—(Matthew 3:4)
12. True—(Matthew 3:4)
13. False—Angels ministered to him (Matthew 4:1, 11)
14. False—He moved to Capernaum (Matthew 4:13)
15. False—He said, "Man shall not live by bread alone" (Matthew 4:4)
16. False—He builds it on sand (Matthew 7:26)
17. False—Nahum prophesied Assyria's destruction (Nahum 3:18)
18. False—He wrote the first five books
19. False—Her story takes place in 1 Samuel
20. True—(Genesis 3:14)

28. Group 7

1. False—She had other children (Mark 6:3)
2. False—It is the fourth book
3. True
4. False—It is the eighth book
5. False—It is the longest book of the New Testament
6. False—It is found in the book of Judges
7. True—(Mark 2:14)
8. True
9. True
10. True—(Genesis 29)
11. True
12. True—(Mark 3:17)
13. False—It means "praise the Lord"
14. True
15. False—Malachi is the last book of the Old Testament
16. True—(Genesis 1:1)
17. True
18. False—Leviticus is the third book
19. False—Acts is the fifth book
20. True—(Numbers 11:31)

29. Group 8

1. True—(Numbers 13:1–16)
2. True—(Numbers 16:28–33)
3. False—They mourned for thirty days (Numbers 20:27–29)
4. True—(Numbers 22:21–33)
5. True—(Numbers 25:7–8)
6. False—He was 123 years old when he died (Numbers 33:39)
7. True—(Numbers 33:39)
8. True—(Philippians 4:16)
9. True—(Proverbs 11:22)
10. True—(Proverbs 20:17)
11. True—(Proverbs 25:1)
12. True—(Proverbs 27:5)
13. True
14. True
15. False—John had the vision (Revelation 1:12)
16. False—The book of Revelation says this (Revelation 1:15)
17. True—(Revelation 1:4)
18. True—(Revelation 11:1–2)
19. True—(Revelation 11:7)
20. True—(Revelation 12:7)

30. Group 9

1. True—(Revelation 16:7)
2. True—(Revelation 17:3)
3. True—(Revelation 18:2)
4. False—It was composed of burning sulfur (Revelation 19:20)
5. True—(Revelation 20:2)
6. False—Twelve angels were at the gates (Revelation 21:12)
7. True—(Revelation 21:19–20)
8. True—(Revelation 3:15–16)
9. False—John had the vision (Revelation 4:6)
10. False—John saw the creature (Revelation 4:7)
11. False—They were holding the four winds (Revelation 7:1)
12. False—A star fell on earth's waters (Revelation 8:10)
13. True—(Romans 10:17)
14. True—(Romans 14:10)

15. False—He says to greet one another with a holy kiss (Romans 16:16)
16. True—(Romans 16:22)
17. True—(Romans 6:23)
18. True—(Romans 8:35–39)
19. False—Elimelech was her husband (Ruth 1:2)
20. False—She was married to Mahlon (Ruth 4:10)

31. Group 10

1. True—(Ruth 1:4)
2. True—(Ruth 4:10)
3. True—(Ruth 4:17)
4. False—He had a throne with purple cushions (Song of Solomon 3:10)
5. False—There are thirty-nine books
6. True—(Titus 3:13)
7. True—(Zechariah 1:8)
8. True—(Zechariah 14:1–4)
9. False—Joshua was the high priest (Zechariah 6:10–11)
10. True

33. Women in the Bible Part 1

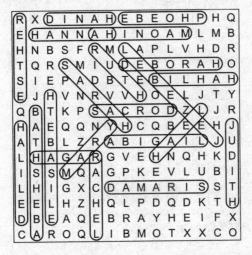

34. Women in the Bible Part 2

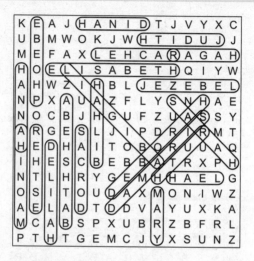

35. Women in the Bible Part 3

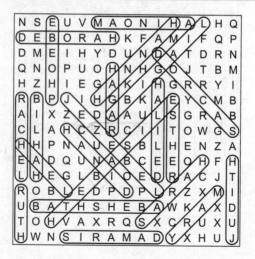

36. Paul's Journeys Part 1

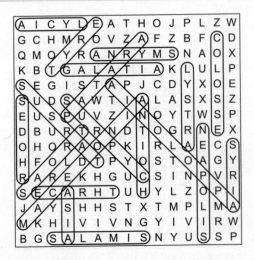

37. Paul's Journeys Part 2

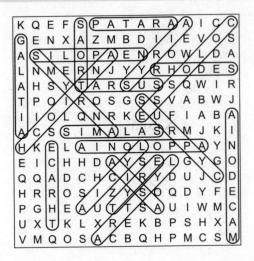

38. Paul's Journeys Part 3

39. Prisoners and Exiles Part 1

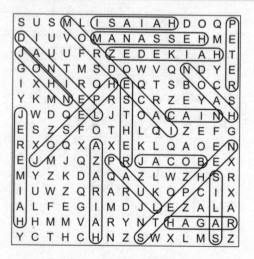

40. Prisoners and Exiles Part 2

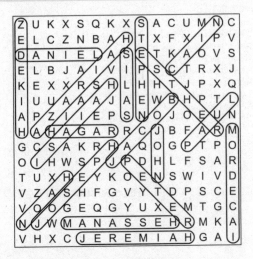

41. Prisoners and Exiles Part 3

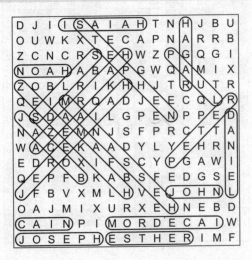

43. Who Is?

1. Job (Job 1:1)
2. Jesus (Revelation 22:16)
3. John the Baptist (Matthew 3:1–3)
4. Jesus (Isaiah 11:1–5)
5. Timothy (1 Timothy 1:2)
6. Lucifer (Isaiah 14:12)
7. Jesus (1 Corinthians 15:45–48)
8. Jesus's disciples (Matthew 5:13)
9. Nimrod (Genesis 10:9)
10. The Pharisees (Matthew 12:24–34)

SECTION 3: THE BIBLE BRILLIANT SECTION

44. Crossword Puzzle

45. Group 1

1. Grasshoppers (Numbers 13:33)
2. Terah (Genesis 11:31)
3. Rams (Exodus 25:3–5)
4. He claimed to be the Son of God (John 19:7)
5. In a dream (Matthew 2:13)
6. Corinthians (2 Corinthians 6:17–18)
7. They cast lots (Jonah 1:7)
8. A Pharisee and a publican (tax collector) (Luke 18:10)
9. His feet (1 Kings 15:23)
10. Malchus (John 18:10)
11. Abib (Deuteronomy 16:1)
12. Philippi (Acts 16:12)
13. The doors of the gate of the city (Judges 16:3)
14. Zadok (1 Kings 1:39)
15. The Ancient of days (Daniel 7:9)
16. Seventy (Judges 8:30)
17. Obadiah
18. Philip's (Acts 21:8)
19. Treasurer (Acts 8:27)
20. "Blessed are the poor in spirit: for theirs is the kingdom of heaven" (Matthew 5:3)
21. Third (Genesis 1:11–13)
22. Philip (John 14:8)
23. Eutychus (Acts 20:9)
24. Singing (Psalm 100:2)
25. Sea of Tiberias (Galilee) (John 6:1; 21:1)
26. Cyprus (Acts 13:4)
27. She destroyed the rest of the royal family (2 Kings 11:1)
28. Elisha (2 Kings 5:10)
29. Three hundred (1 Kings 11:3)
30. It doesn't list a number (Matthew 2:1–12)
31. Tentmaker (Acts 18:2–3)
32. Og (Deuteronomy 3:11)
33. He tossed a piece of wood into the water (Exodus 15:23–25)
34. Almighty God (Genesis 17:1)
35. Sheets (linen garments, NKJV) and garments (Judges 14:12)
36. Samaria (Acts 8:12–14)
37. Paul's (Acts 19:12)
38. No, they were not ashamed (Genesis 2:25)
39. 120,000 (Jonah 4:11)
40. He was baptized (Acts 9:18)
41. Thou shall not commit adultery (Exodus 20:14)
42. Three (Deuteronomy 4:41–43)
43. A stone like a great millstone (Revelation 18:21)
44. Zarephath (1 Kings 17:9–23)
45. Ezekiel (Ezekiel 3:2)
46. Despising God (1 Thessalonians 4:7–8)
47. Julius (Acts 27:1)
48. Samuel (1 Samuel 15:22)
49. Righteous and blameless (Genesis 6:9)
50. He was lowered in a basket by the city wall (Acts 9:23–25)

46. Group 2

1. Bezaleel (Exodus 31:2–3)
2. Gravel (Proverbs 20:17)
3. Foolishness (Proverbs 22:15)
4. 127 years old (Genesis 23:1)
5. Ahijah (1 Kings 11:30–31)
6. Bread and wine (Genesis 14:18)
7. A thirty-foot flying roll (Zechariah 5:1–4)
8. She was his grandmother (2 Timothy 1:5)
9. The coming of the Messiah (Daniel 9:20–27)
10. Thirteen (1 Kings 7:1)

11. Which disciple was the greatest (Luke 22:24–30)
12. Rivers and fountains of waters turned to blood (Revelation 16:4)
13. Asher (Luke 2:36)
14. Ai (Joshua 7:5–12)
15. Onyx (Exodus 28:9)
16. Philippi (Acts 16:11–14)
17. Ammonites (Judges 11:9–11)
18. Fifty denarii (Luke 7:41)
19. Locusts (Exodus 10:4; Revelation 9:1–4)
20. Agabus (Acts 21:10–11)
21. Annas (John 18:13)
22. Eight years (Judges 12:13–14)
23. A lion, a bear, a leopard, and a dreadful and terrible beast (Daniel 7:3–7)
24. Barnabas (Acts 13:4)
25. "The lost sheep of the house of Israel" (Matthew 10:5–6)
26. Seventy (Exodus 15:27)
27. Rubies (Proverbs 8:11)
28. Four (Genesis 2:10)
29. Jewels of silver and gold and raiment (Exodus 3:22)
30. On earth (Revelation 5:10)
31. The wife of Phinehas (1 Samuel 4:19)
32. Elymas (Acts 13:8)
33. Jesus (Mark 1:14)
34. Ishmaelites (Genesis 37:28)
35. The sick (James 5:15)
36. Joseph (Genesis 41:45)
37. In the valley of Sorek (Judges 16:4)
38. Joab (2 Samuel 14:22–23)
39. Onesiphorus (2 Timothy 1:16)
40. Each would sit on one of the twelve thrones and judge the twelve tribes of Israel (Matthew 19:28)
41. That it will sprout again (Job 14:7)
42. Mist rose from the earth (Genesis 2:5–6)
43. Angels (Revelation 5:11–12)
44. Purim (Esther 9:24–26)
45. Half (Luke 19:8)
46. Rebekah (Genesis 24:14–19)
47. Eighty-four years old (Luke 2:37)
48. John (John 6:48)
49. A young goat and unleavened bread (Judges 6:19)
50. Machpelah (Genesis 23:19)

47. Group 3

1. Household idols (Genesis 31:19)
2. A crown (Proverbs 12:4)
3. Psalm 58 (Psalm 58:8)
4. Daniel (Judges 13:25)
5. To keep them from the Egyptians who thought shepherds were an abomination (Genesis 46:34)
6. A priest (Luke 10:31)
7. Numbers (Numbers 22:22–35)
8. To know understanding (Proverbs 4:1)
9. Fish and honeycomb (Luke 24:42)
10. 110 years old (Genesis 50:22)
11. Make one hair white or black (Matthew 5:36)
12. Every creature of God (1 Timothy 4:5)
13. With the fruit of his mouth (Proverbs 18:20)
14. Sun, moon, and stars (Genesis 1:14–18)
15. Bethlehem (1 Samuel 17:58)
16. A scorpion (Luke 11:12)
17. "In sanctification and honour" (1 Thessalonians 4:4)
18. Thirty (Judges 14:11)
19. Moses (Psalm 90:1)
20. 350 years (Genesis 9:28)

21. Trumpets and cymbals (Ezra 3:10)
22. 147 (Genesis 47:28)
23. Simeon (Genesis 42:24)
24. Isaiah (Isaiah 20:2–3)
25. Seventeen (Jeremiah 32:9)
26. Goats (Song of Solomon 4:1)
27. Cain's fruit of the ground (Genesis 4:3)
28. Summer (Matthew 24:32)
29. Those who do God's commandments (Revelation 22:14)
30. Lying (Proverbs 21:6)
31. Blue (Exodus 28:31)
32. Prevails with God (Genesis 32:28)
33. Build a battlement (guard rail) around the roof (Deuteronomy 22:8)
34. Hosea (Hosea 11:1)
35. A wall fell on them (1 Kings 20:30)
36. 666 talents (about 39,960 pounds) (1 Kings 10:14)
37. Benhadad (2 Kings 8:15)
38. A Hittite (Ezekiel 16:3)
39. Pray for one another (James 5:16)
40. Dorcas (Acts 9:36)
41. 1 Samuel (1 Samuel 17)
42. Gold (Proverbs 16:16)
43. Tongues of fire (Acts 2:3)
44. Those without fins and scales (Deuteronomy 14:9)
45. Reuben (Genesis 30:14)
46. He was a man of war (1 Chronicles 28:3)
47. Moses (Exodus 2:21)
48. Nebuchadnezzar (Daniel 4:1–11)
49. Jehoshaphat (2 Kings 9:2)
50. Hebrew, Greek, and Latin (John 19:19–20)

48. Group 4

1. Saul (Acts 9:17–18)
2. Moses and Aaron (Numbers 1:46)
3. John the Baptist (Luke 1:41)
4. Thirty years old (2 Samuel 5:4)
5. Joshua (Joshua 24:15)
6. Be faithful until death (Revelation 2:10)
7. Psalms (Psalm 117; 119)
8. One hundred years old (Genesis 21:5)
9. Four (Genesis 2:10)
10. Six cubits and a span (over nine feet tall) (1 Samuel 17:4)
11. Both Peter (Matthew 16:23) and Satan (Luke 4:8)
12. Antioch (Acts 11:26)
13. Love (Romans 13:10)
14. Simon of Cyrene (Matthew 27:32; Mark 15:21)
15. Levi (Exodus 2:1)
16. The new Jerusalem (Revelation 3:12)
17. Abimelech (Genesis 26:1–9)
18. Midian (Exodus 2:15)
19. Keturah (Genesis 25:1)
20. Mary Magdalene; Joanna; and Mary, the mother of James (Luke 24:10)
21. Aaron (Exodus 7:7)
22. Ruth and Esther
23. Simon and Andrew (Mark 1:16)
24. Samson (Judges 14:5–9)
25. Levi (Deuteronomy 18:2)
26. The bones of Joseph (Exodus 13:19)
27. Circumcision (Genesis 17:10)
28. Gideon (Judges 8:32)
29. Bethlehem (Luke 2:4)
30. Joseph (Genesis 46:20)
31. Pharaoh's daughter (Exodus 2:10)

32. His brother Aaron (Exodus 4:14–16)
33. A serpent (Genesis 3:1–4) and a donkey (Numbers 22:28–30)
34. His father-in-law, Jethro (Exodus 3:1)
35. Twelve baskets full (Matthew 14:20)
36. Job (Job 1:8)
37. Seven (Luke 8:2)
38. Ninety-nine years old (Genesis 17:24)
39. Matthias (Acts 1:26)
40. Nod (Genesis 4:16)
41. Satan (Matthew 4:4)
42. Four days (John 11:39)
43. Nine (Matthew 27:46)
44. His disciples (John 4:2)
45. Moab (Deuteronomy 34:6)
46. Seth (Genesis 4:25)
47. Pearls (Revelation 21:21)
48. Enoch (Genesis 4:17)
49. None (Romans 3:10)
50. 930 years (Genesis 5:5)

49. Fulfilled Prophecies about Jesus

1. Matthew 1:22–23 and Luke 1:27
2. Luke 3:3–6
3. Matthew 1:20 and Galatians 4:4
4. Matthew 3:16–17
5. Matthew 2:1 and Luke 2:4–6
6. Matthew 27:37 and Mark 11:7–11
7. Luke 1:33 and Hebrews 1:8–12
8. Luke 3:33 and Hebrews 7:14
9. Matthew 1:1 and Romans 9:5
10. Luke 4:18–19
11. Matthew 2:14–15
12. Matthew 27:38
13. Luke 1:32–33 and Romans 1:3
14. John 1:11 and John 7:5
15. Matthew 1:23
16. Matthew 27:34 and John 19:28–30
17. Acts 3:20–22
18. Matthew 2:23
19. Matthew 21:16
20. Matthew 26:67
21. John 15:24–25
22. Luke 23:35
23. Luke 3:34
24. Romans 5:6–8
25. Matthew 13:10–15, 34–35
26. Matthew 26:14–16 and Luke 22:47–48
27. John 19:33–36
28. John 20:25–27
29. Mark 14:57–58
30. Mark 15:4–5
31. Matthew 27:35–36 and Luke 23:34
32. Matthew 27:46
33. John 19:34
34. Matthew 28:2–7 and Acts 2:22–32
35. Mark 16:19 and Luke 24:51
36. Matthew 22:44 and Mark 16:19

50. The Fast 100

1. Garden of Gethsemane (Matthew 26:36)
2. Sleeping (Jonah 1:5)
3. Potiphar (Genesis 37:36)
4. Egypt (Matthew 2:13–14)
5. The walls fell down (Joshua 6:20)
6. Canaan (Genesis 17:8)
7. An earthquake (Acts 16:26)
8. Ten (Exodus 7:14–12:30)
9. Wisdom (1 Kings 3:9)
10. With animal sacrifices (Leviticus 4)
11. A burning bush (Exodus 3:2)

12. The kingdom of God and his righteousness (Matthew 6:33)
13. Rachel (Genesis 29:30)
14. Without ceasing (1 Thessalonians 5:17)
15. The ark of the covenant (Deuteronomy 10:8)
16. In your closet with the door shut (Matthew 6:6)
17. The breath of life (Genesis 2:7)
18. John (Revelation 1:1)
19. Three days (John 1:17)
20. Ishmael (Genesis 16:15)
21. Making a false idol, a golden calf (Deuteronomy 9:15–16)
22. Abram (Genesis 12:1)
23. A pillar of cloud and a pillar of fire (Exodus 13:21)
24. Thirty years old (Luke 3:2)
25. A donkey (Numbers 22:28)
26. Leah (Genesis 29)
27. Moses (Exodus 14:21)
28. Barabbas (Matthew 27:21)
29. Sarai (Genesis 11:29)
30. John the Baptist (Matthew 3:13)
31. Gabriel (Luke 1:26)
32. Rebekah (Genesis 24:67)
33. The disciples (Matthew 8:26)
34. In the earth (Matthew 25:25)
35. Rachel (Genesis 29:28)
36. Hannah (1 Samuel 1:20)
37. Swaddling clothes (Luke 2:7)
38. Michal (1 Samuel 18:20–26)
39. "You are the Christ, the Son of the living God" (Matthew 16:16)
40. The bridegroom (Matthew 25:1)
41. Joseph (Luke 1:27)
42. Ruth (Ruth 1:16)
43. Potiphar's wife (Genesis 39:14)
44. He forced it to move on its belly and eat dust (Genesis 3:14)
45. Zipporah (Exodus 2:21)
46. Judas (Luke 22:48)
47. In the knowledge of good and evil (Genesis 3:22)
48. To take no thought for it (Matthew 6:34)
49. Jacob (Genesis 32:28)
50. Not judge them and treat them impartially (James 2:1–4)
51. In the Jordan River (Mark 1:9)
52. Peter (Matthew 16:18)
53. He draws nigh (near) to us (James 4:8)
54. Joseph (Genesis 41:41)
55. Easter Sunday
56. "He that is without sin among you, let him first cast a stone at her" (John 8:7)
57. Delilah (Judges 16:6)
58. Mary (Luke 1:46)
59. Satan (Matthew 4:3)
60. Saul, who became Paul (Acts 8:22)
61. Mother of all living (Genesis 3:20)
62. Esther (Esther 7:3)
63. Jezebel (1 Kings 19:2)
64. He climbed a tree (Luke 19:4)
65. Esau (Genesis 25:34)
66. Jochebed (Exodus 6:20)
67. Daniel (Daniel 6:23)
68. Lot's wife (Genesis 19:6)
69. Orpah (Ruth 1:4)
70. To hide his nakedness (Genesis 3:10)
71. Daniel (Daniel 1:17)
72. God with us (Matthew 1:23)
73. Gopher wood (Genesis 6:14)
74. The angel of the Lord (Matthew 1:20–21)
75. He believed God was on his side (1 Samuel 17:46)
76. The Sermon on the Mount (Matthew 5:1)
77. Almonds (Numbers 17:8)
78. A dove (Luke 3:22)
79. God the Father (Matthew 3:17)
80. They were cast into the lake of fire (Revelation 20:15)
81. Sea of Galilee (John 6:1–19)

82. He clothed them (Genesis 3:21)
83. Gomer (Hosea 1:3)
84. Hagar (Genesis 16:15)
85. He was angry (Jonah 4:1)
86. Joshua (Deuteronomy 34:9)
87. As a little child (Luke 18:17)
88. He was thrown into the lions'
    den (Daniel 6:16)
89. His brother (Luke 15:25)
90. God the Father (Matthew 3:17)
91. Chief tax collector (Luke 19:2)
92. Interpreting dreams (Genesis
    41:12)

93. To keep the meaning from those
    who would not understand
    (Matthew 13:13)
94. Grain (Genesis 41:57)
95. Satan (Matthew 4:9)
96. He was lowered through the roof
    (Mark 2:4)
97. Thomas (John 20:28)
98. Benjamin (Genesis 42:4)
99. Cherubim (angels) and a flaming
    sword (Genesis 3:24)
100. Mustard seed (Matthew 13:31–
    32)

51. Who Asked?

1. C (Genesis 4:9)
2. B (Genesis 15:2)
3. C (Genesis 18:25)
4. A (Exodus 5:22)
5. D (Genesis 15:8)
6. A (Jeremiah 15:18)

7. B (Habakkuk 1:3)
8. A (Numbers 16:22)
9. C (Ezekiel 11:13)
10. C (Exodus 3:13)
11. B (Job 40:4)
12. D (1 Samuel 23:2)

52. Hearing from God

1. C (Genesis 6:14)
2. D (Genesis 12:1)
3. D (Exodus 28:1)
4. D (1 Kings 12:20)

5. C (1 Kings 17:17–24)
6. B (Exodus 6:6)
7. B (Numbers 25:11–12)
8. C (Genesis 37:5–8)

53. Bible Brilliant Level

1. C (John 11:35)
2. B (Job 29:6)
3. C (Acts 9:36–41)
4. A (Joshua 6:17–25)
5. A (Genesis 29:11)
6. B (Judges 9:1–6)
7. B (Judges 14:5–6; 1 Samuel
    17:36; 1 Chronicles 11:22)
8. B (Judges 3:31)
9. D (Daniel 4:33)
10. A (Exodus 26:14)
11. C (2 Kings 2:20)

12. D (Luke 1:1–4; Acts 1:1)
13. C (1 Samuel 14:50)
14. B (2 Kings 18:4)
15. C (Revelation 3:9)
16. C (Ecclesiastes 2:2)
17. D (Exodus 12:40)
18. B (Revelation 21:12)
19. C (Isaiah 38:5)
20. C (Matthew 13:55; Luke 6:16;
    John 14:22; Acts 5:37; 9:11;
    15:32)

54. Anything Goes

1. D (Genesis 7:13)

2. D (Judges 4:4)

3. B (Luke 1:26–31)
4. B (Genesis 6:16)
5. A (2 Corinthians 11:33)
6. A (Genesis 41:27)
7. C (Acts 5:1–11)
8. C (2 Kings 9:10)
9. A (1 Samuel 4:21)
10. C (Psalm 56:8)
11. D (Ruth 1:2–4)
12. C (2 Kings 21:1)
13. C (1 Kings 10:1–7)
14. A (Matthew 3:4)
15. B (Acts 9:9)
16. C (1 Kings 3:25)
17. C (John 3:2)
18. A (Acts 12:5–17)
19. B (Genesis 6:10, 18; 1 Peter 3:20)
20. D (1 Samuel 25:14–42)
21. A (Daniel 5:2)
22. B (Philemon 10–18)
23. C (1 Kings 21:1–4)
24. A (Genesis 20:3)
25. C (Genesis 8:8–12)

26. B (Esther 9:13)
27. B (Genesis 40:22)
28. A (Esther 2:21)
29. C (1 Kings 10:21)
30. C (1 Kings 11:4)
31. A (2 Corinthians 11:25)
32. B (Acts 23:8)
33. A (1 Chronicles 3:10)
34. B (2 Chronicles 11:21)
35. A (Exodus 26:14)
36. C (1 Kings 2:20)
37. B (Genesis 9)
38. D (Luke 1:1–4; Acts 1:1)
39. C (1 Samuel 14:50)
40. B (2 Kings 18:4)
41. C (Revelation 3:9)
42. C (Ecclesiastes 2:2)
43. D (Exodus 12:40)
44. B (Revelation 21:12)
45. C (Isaiah 38:5)
46. C (Matthew 13:55; Luke 6:16; John 14:22; Acts 5:37; 9:11; 15:32)

55. Royalty

1. C (1 Kings 11:3)
2. A (1 Samuel 9)
3. D (1 Kings 11:7)
4. B (Acts 18:3)
5. D (Exodus 32:4)

6. B (Luke 23:8)
7. A (2 Chronicles 36:11–21)
8. B (1 Kings 7:13–14)
9. D (Daniel 5:1–5)
10. C (Numbers 21:9)

56. Firsts

1. A (Matthew 4:18–20)
2. B (Judges 3:9–10)
3. C (Genesis 4:6)
4. A (Genesis 8:20)
5. C (Genesis 24:65–67)

6. D (Genesis 41:42)
7. B (Genesis 4:2)
8. D (Genesis 14:17–18)
9. A (Genesis 29:9)
10. D (Acts 13:1–13)

57. Random Bible Trivia

1. B (Acts 2:14–42)
2. A (Revelation 3:16)
3. C (Mark 2:14)
4. C (Matthew 26:75)

5. B (Numbers 20:11)
6. C (Daniel 7:9)
7. A (Exodus 16:13)
8. A (2 Kings 6:18–23)

9. B (Acts 17:28)
10. C (Ephesians 5:14)
11. B (1 Samuel 19:10)
12. A (Genesis 19:1)
13. B (Matthew 26:36)
14. C (Exodus 7:20)
15. A (Matthew 12:27)
16. D (Ezekiel 1:1)
17. D (John 11:43)

18. C (Genesis 17:15)
19. C (Matthew 8:24)
20. A (Genesis 26:34)
21. B (2 Chronicles 24:25–26)
22. A (Genesis 41:45)
23. B (John 2:1–11)
24. C (Luke 1:43)
25. D (Luke 2:36–37)

58. Who Is God?

1. Genesis 18:14; Luke 18:27; Revelation 19:6
2. Deuteronomy 33:27; Psalm 90:2; Jeremiah 10:10
3. 1 Kings 8:22–27; Jeremiah 23:24; Psalm 102:25–27; Revelation 22:13
4. Exodus 3:13–14; Psalm 50:10–12; Colossians 1:16
5. Psalm 139:7–12
6. James 1:17; 1 John 1:4–5
7. 2 Samuel 7:22; Isaiah 46:9–11
8. Psalm 139:2–6; Isaiah 40:13–14
9. Psalm 102:25–27; Hebrews 1:10–12
10. Leviticus 19:2; 1 Peter 1:15
11. Proverbs 3:19; Romans 16:26–27; 1 Timothy 1:17
12. Deuteronomy 32:4; Psalm 11:7; Psalm 119:137
13. Psalm 31:5; John 14:6; John 17:3; Titus 1:1–2
14. Deuteronomy 7:9; Psalm 89:1–8
15. Exodus 34:6; Psalm 103:8; 1 Peter 5:10
16. Psalm 25:8; Psalm 34:8; Mark 10:18
17. Deuteronomy 4:31; Psalm 103:8–17; Daniel 9:9; Hebrews 2:17
18. John 4:24
19. John 3:16; Romans 5:8; 1 John 4:8
20. Matthew 28:19; 2 Corinthians 13:14

SECTION 4: THE BONUS SECTION

59. The Sixty Hardest Questions

1. Methuselah, 969 (Genesis 5:27); Jared, 962 (Genesis 5:20); Adam, 960 (Genesis 5:5); Noah, 950 (Genesis 9:29); Seth 912 (Genesis 5:8); Kenan, 910 (Genesis 5:14); Enosh, 905 (Genesis 5:11)
2. Ehud (Judges 3:15)
3. Joshua (Joshua 12:9–24)
4. Sarah, 127 (Genesis 23:1)

5. Joseph, who died at age 110 (Genesis 50:22)
6. Zedekiah and Ahab (Jeremiah 29:22)
7. At the baptism of Jesus (Matthew 3:17), at the transfiguration (Matthew 17:5), and shortly before Jesus went to the cross (John 12:28)
8. Three years (Exodus 7:7)
9. Joseph (Genesis 41:14)
10. Saul (1 Chronicles 10:8–10)
11. A sheep (Genesis 4:2–4)
12. Mahlon (Ruth 1:4–5; 4:10)
13. Thirty-seven; she died at age 127 and gave birth at age 90 (Genesis 23:1)
14. Twelve (Luke 8:41–42)
15. Lamech (Genesis 4:23)
16. Joseph (Exodus 13:19)
17. Noah (Genesis 8:20)
18. Lydia (Acts 16:14–15)
19. Acts, James, and 3 John
20. Joseph (Genesis 50:26)
21. Isaac (Genesis 24:11–67), Jacob (Genesis 29:1–29), and Moses (Exodus 2:15–21)
22. Zenas (Titus 3:13)
23. Manasseh (2 Kings 21:1)
24. Er (Genesis 38:7)
25. Bow and arrow, mace, sling, sword, ax, club, dagger, and spear (1 Samuel 17:45)
26. Stephen (Acts 6:7–8)
27. Zimri (1 Kings 16:15)
28. Miriam (Exodus 15:21)
29. Gamaliel (Acts 22:3)
30. Dinah (Genesis 34:1)
31. Othniel (Judges 3:9–10)
32. Philip (Mark 6:17)
33. John the Baptist (John 1:35–37, 40)
34. Sadducees (Acts 23:8)
35. Lahmi (1 Chronicles 20:5)
36. "Where art thou" (to Adam) (Genesis 3:9)
37. The ostrich (Leviticus 11:16)
38. Abram (Genesis 14:13)
39. Aaron, the brother of Moses (Luke 1:5)
40. Rachel, while giving birth to Benjamin (Genesis 35:16–19), and the wife of Phinehas, while giving birth to Ichabod (1 Samuel 4:19–22)
41. Green (Genesis 1:30)
42. Enoch (Jude 1:14)
43. Felix (Acts 23:23), Festus (Acts 25:1), and Fortunatus (1 Corinthians 16:17)
44. Malachi, in which forty-seven of the fifty-five verses are God speaking
45. Havilah (Genesis 2:11–12)
46. Eli the high priest (1 Samuel 4:17–18)
47. Zeruiah and Abigail (1 Chronicles 2:13–16)
48. Twenty-five (Numbers 8:24–25)
49. The king of Nineveh (Jonah 3:7–8)
50. Judges (Judges 5:10)
51. James (Acts 12:1–2)
52. Joash (2 Chronicles 24:1)
53. Ruth (Ruth 4:21–22; Matthew 1:5–6)
54. Gideon (Judges 7:4–7)
55. Ur (Genesis 11:28), Ai (Joshua 7:2), On (Genesis 41:45), Ar (Numbers 21:15), Uz (Job 1:1), No (Ezekiel 30:15)
56. The feeding of the five thousand (Matthew 14:13–21; Mark 6:32–44; Luke 9:12–17; John 6:1–14)
57. Caesar Augustus
58. Moses (Exodus 34:28) and Elijah (1 Kings 19:8)
59. Elijah raised the widow's son (1 Kings 17:17–24), Elijah raised the son of the Shunammite (2 Kings 4:18–37),

an unnamed man was raised after his body was set upon the bones of Elisha (2 Kings 13:20–21), Jesus raised the son of a widow (Luke 7:11–15), Jesus raised the daughter of Jarius (Luke 8:41–42, 49–56), Jesus raised Lazarus (John 11:1–46), Jesus himself was resurrected (Matthew 28), many dead saints arose out of their graves after the crucifixion of Jesus (Matthew 27:51–53), Peter raised Tabitha (Dorcas) (Acts 9:36–51), and Paul raised Eutychus (Acts 20:9–12)

60. When he fed the five thousand with five loaves of bread and two fish (Matthew 14:15–21), when the money to pay taxes was found in the mouth of a fish (Matthew 17:27), when Peter was told by Jesus to let down his fishing nets again and the nets filled with fish (Luke 5:4–11), and when Jesus told the disciples to cast their net on the right side of the boat and the net was filled with fish (John 21:4–11)

Timothy E. Parker is a Guinness World Records Puzzle Master and an ordained minister. He entertains over twenty million puzzle solvers as the senior crossword puzzle editor of the Universal line of crosswords and assorted puzzle games. He is the author of more than thirty books and the founder of Bible Brilliant. CNN calls his puzzles "Smart games for smart people," and he has created custom games for companies including Microsoft, Disney, Coca-Cola, Nike, Warner Bros., and Comcast. For more Bible puzzles and quizzes, go to www.BibleBrilliant.com.